# Devil In My Headlights

Songs about breaking free, letting loose, healing, and loving the one you're with.

ISBN: 978-1-946195-45-6
FuzionPress

# Table of Contents

Photos by Lisa Nebenzahl

# Introduction

I have been writing and performing music for forty years. I started listening to music at a young age. I listened to Joe and Eddy, the Righteous Brothers, Peter, Paul, and Mary, and a little later Barbara Streisand as I ironed every Saturday morning. I sang at the top of my lungs, knowing every word. I was the third child of five in a home with alcoholism and mental illness and became "invisible" when I was very young. The music kept me company and made me feel like I was not alone and there was more to life than what I saw around me. It was exciting to feel the melodies and the rhythm inside me. I started listening to Billie Holiday, Nina Simone, Quincy Jones, and Eddie Harris. Then I discovered Emmy Lou Harris, Waylon Jennings, and Rita Coolidge. I loved how the music transformed me, and the world around me. I taught myself piano and a friend gave me a guitar and taught me a few chords. I started writing my own songs hearing little whispers of songs from my past. I went back to college and studied music in all its forms. Music became my "home." I have performed in restaurants/bars, theatres, cafes, and coffee shops. I have taught piano, guitar and voice for seventeen years. My adult students have performed in We Fest, house concerts throughout the country, and music festivals. I have produced two albums of original music and performed my songs in my one-woman show "Merica's Story." My songs have been performed in plays I've written, sung at weddings and funerals, and used as background music in educational videos.

The songs in this book are eclectic: some are folk, some blues with a little jazz thrown in, some country, and some light rock. They tell stories of my life. From "Devil in my Headlights", a country tune about taking a risk and jumping on the stage to perform, to poignant songs like "Bright Eyes" dealing with a loved one's drug addiction, to "Little Bird" a song about finding your own voice and "I Met Him on a Touring ship" a story of love and romance. This book contains different styles of guitar music, a little classical flare, and soft rock, songs using the whole neck of the guitar. Some songs have tablature and some just the notes. I hope you enjoy the journey of playing my songs and experiencing all they have to offer.

I also have a piano book called "Little Bird." My piano songs are a combination of folk, spiritual, and a little new age thrown in.

Warm thoughts,
Helen Lapakko

Helen can be contacted at merica.p7@gmail.com

# 3 O'Clock In The Morning

Helen Lapakko

Lyrics:

It was 3 o' clock____ ____ in the mor ning_____ when I got_____ your____ call_____ It was 3 o' clock_____ in the mor ning_____ you were hur tin' and read-y to fall ___ are you go ___ ne could you be go ne ___ what did I do wrong ___ could you be go ne ___

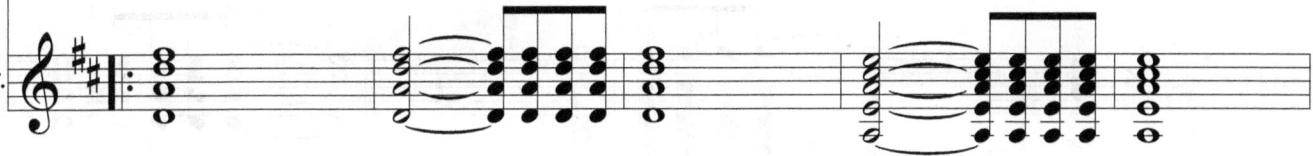

You said "Can you _____ come o _____ ver _____ and
We _____ sat there _____ for _____ ho - urs _____ we

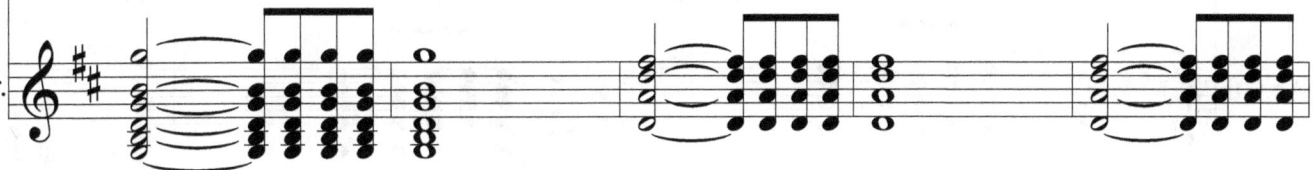

hold _____ my _____ hand" _____ you said "Can you _____
talked the _____ night a way _____ We _____ sat there _____

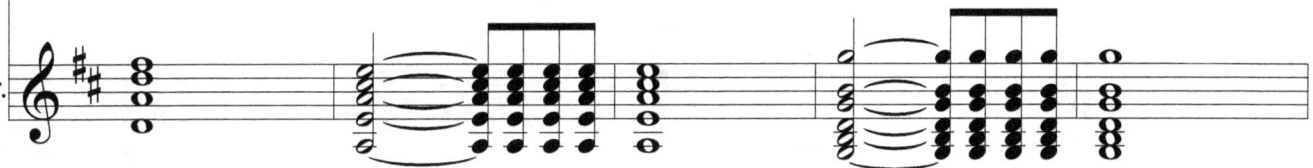

_____ come o _____ ver _____ I real ly _____ need a
_____ for _____ ho - urs _____ there was so _____ much to

friend" _____ When I _____ got _____ there _____
say _____ Then I _____ had to _____ go _____

9

Lyrics:

I sat down by your side
I said go-od ni-ght

When I got there I held you
Then I had to go you real-ly

while you cried Are you gone
seemed all right

could you be go ne

Lyrics: what did I do wrong _____ could you be gone

# A Summer's Journey

Helen Lapakko

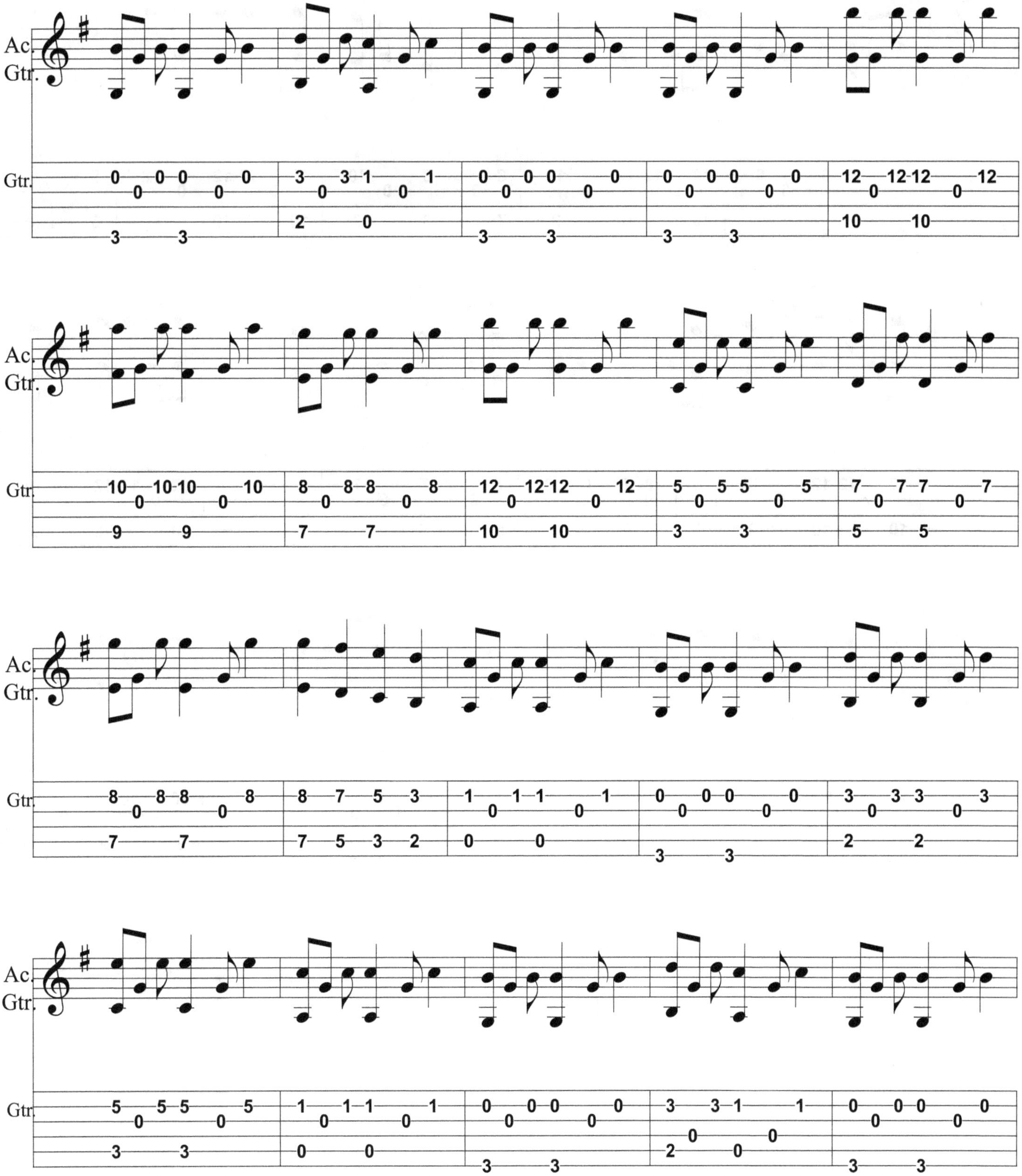
Ac. Gtr.
Gtr.
Ac. Gtr.
Gtr.
Ac. Gtr.
Gtr.
Ac. Gtr.
Gtr.

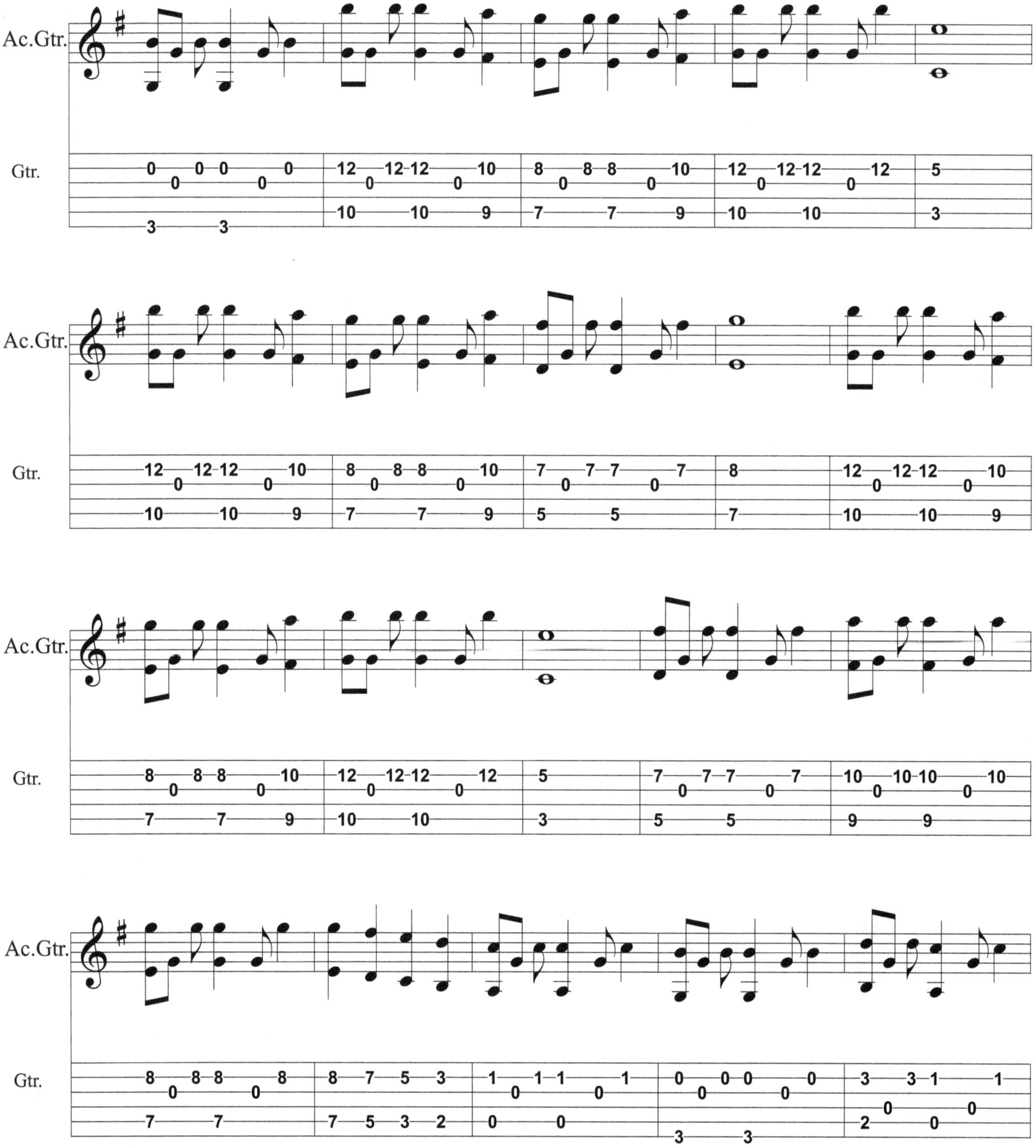
Ac.Gtr.
Gtr.

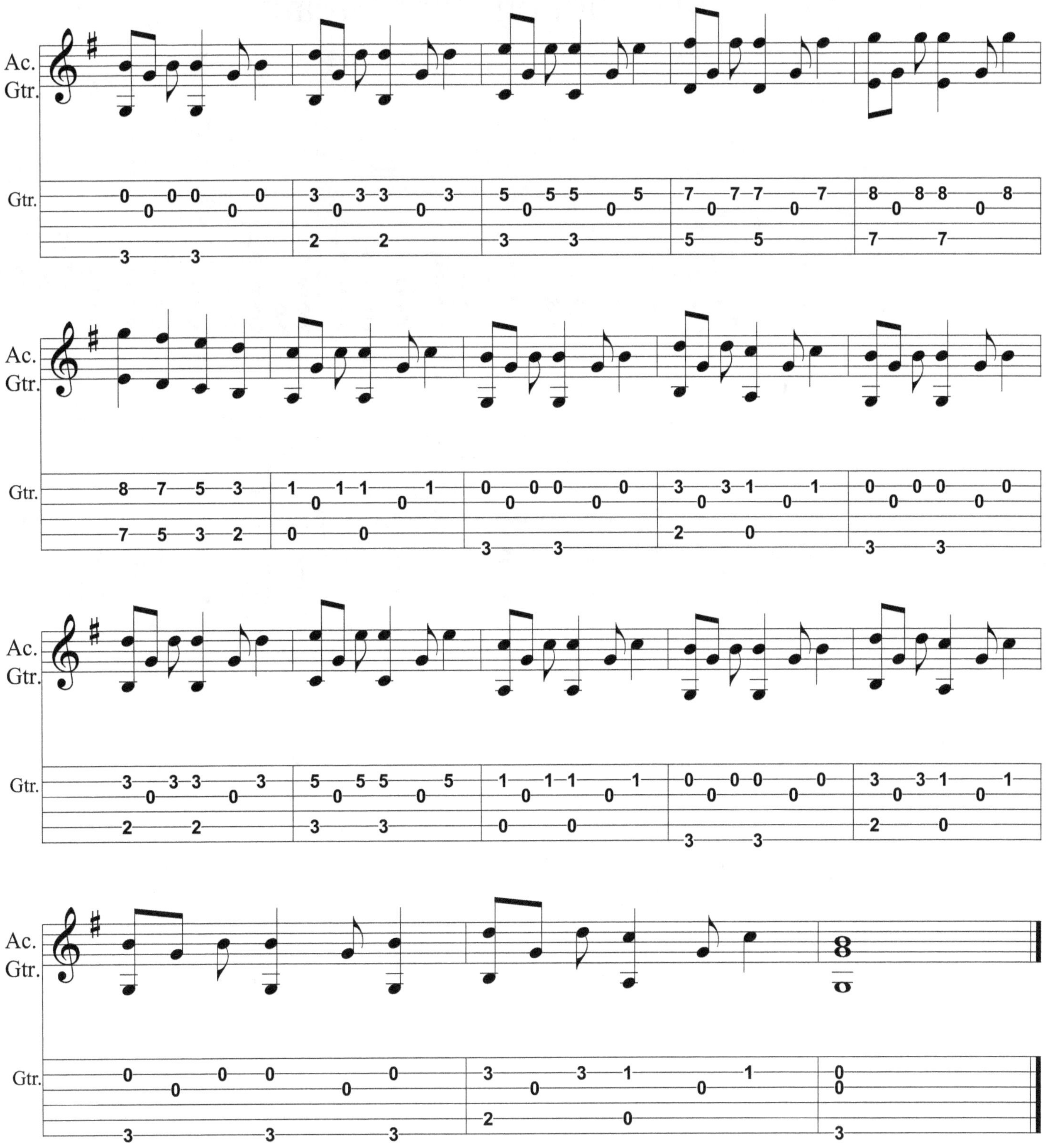
Ac. Gtr.
Gtr.
Ac. Gtr.
Gtr.
Ac. Gtr.
Gtr.
Ac. Gtr.
Gtr.

# Alcohol on Your Breath

Helen Lapakko

Lyrics:

Al - co - hol on your breath blood - shot eyes you're just drink-in' your self to death

When I first met you
Well you first kept tell - in' me

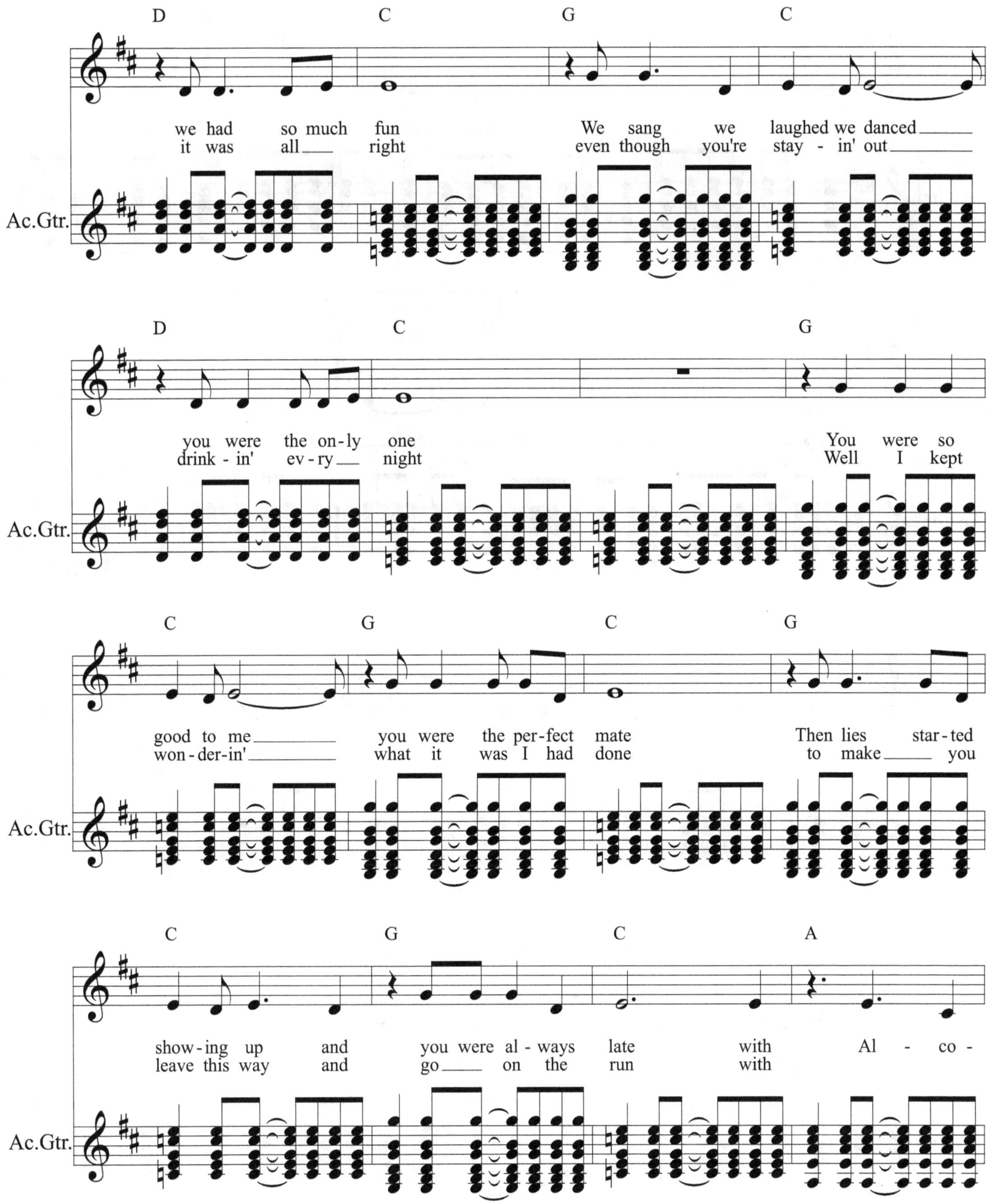
D C G C
we had so much fun We sang we laughed we danced
it was all right even though you're stay - in' out
Ac.Gtr.
D C G
you were the on-ly one You were so
drink - in' ev - ry night Well I kept
Ac.Gtr.
C G C G
good to me you were the per-fect mate Then lies star-ted
won - der-in' what it was I had done to make you
Ac.Gtr.
C G C A
show - ing up and you were al - ways late with Al - co -
leave this way and go on the run with
Ac.Gtr.

D A D A
hol on your breath blood - shot
Ac.Gtr.
1 2
D A D D G
eyes you're just drink-in' your self to death self to death Why don't you
Ac.Gtr.
C D C G
quit stop all that run-nin' a - roound can't you see the
Ac.Gtr.
C D C
pain I'm in e-ven though I don't make a sound
Ac.Gtr.

Don't you know that ev-ry-one_____ they're gon-na say good - bye

They don't want to see you high no they're sick of see-in' you cry with

Al - co - hol on your breath

blood - shot eyes_____ you're just drink-in' your self to death_____

19

drink-in' your self to death _____ drink-in' your self to death

Ac.Gtr.

# Arms Reaching to the Sky

Helen Lapakko

Lyrics:

I see a
As she grows

lit-tle girl____ arms reach-ing to the sky I see the lon-li-ness____
old-er her____ arms fall____ to her sides The sadness is still__ there____

hid-ing in her eyes Her long brown hair blows____ in the
hid-den in her eyes She makes lots of friends run - nin' the

21

breeze · · · · · I see the lit-tle scabs _____ cov-er-ing her knees
street · · · · · Hi-ding her ey-es from _____ ev-ry one she meets

Ac.Gtr.

C · · · · · G · · · · · C · · · · · D

Now she _____ moves so fast · · · · · want-ing some-one to see
Now she's a wo - man _____ · · · · · want-ing to _____ be seen

Ac.Gtr.

Am · · · · · Em · · · · · Am · · · · · D · · · · · C

a per-son to watch her as _____ · · · · · she climbs her _____ trees · · · · · But when she
Some-one who will look in side _____ · · · · · and see her beau - ty · · · · · She learned as

Ac.Gtr.

G · · · · · C · · · · · D · · · · · Am · · · · · Em

turns a - round · · · · · no-one is there _____ · · · · · No arms to catch her as _____
a little girl · · · · · how to hide _____ · · · · · all those _____ feel-ings she _____

Ac.Gtr.

22

Lyrics:

she falls through the air
has ____ in her eyes

What is she look-in' for ____ what does she need why is she al-ways ____

look-ing at me

Love does-n't come eas - y    her hearts hid-den in the

trees        wait-ing for some-one who    sees what she sees

Some-one who knows a - bout___    the se-crets that lie deep    The ones hid-den

in her eyes    She was told to    keep

Lyrics: What is she look-in' for ___ what does she need why is she al-ways ___ look-in' at me why is she al-ways ___ look-in' ___ at me ___

# Black Tears

Helen Lapakko

Lyrics:
Black tears are fal-ling from my eyes It's like I'm wear-ing a dis -

27

It's like I'm wear-ing a dis - guise

Then red starts flash-ing in ___ my dreams
I sing my songs ___ but no-one hears

so man-y words I want to scre-am Black tears are
the tune it falls on ___ deaf ___ ears

28

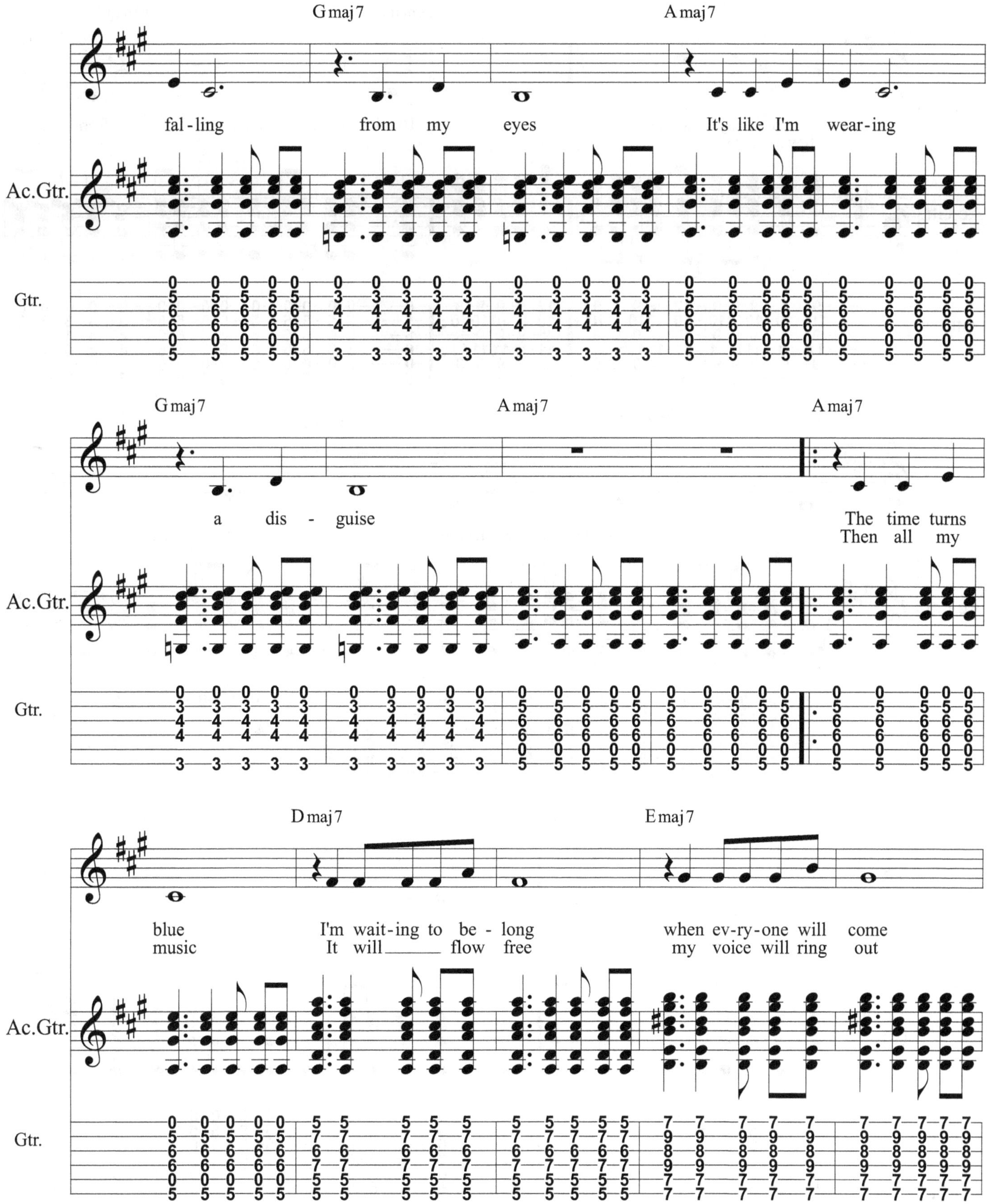
G maj 7
A maj 7
fal - ling from my eyes It's like I'm wear - ing
Ac.Gtr.
Gtr.
G maj 7
A maj 7
A maj 7
a dis - guise
The time turns
Then all my
Ac.Gtr.
Gtr.
D maj 7
E maj 7
blue I'm wait - ing to be - long when ev - ry - one will come
music It will flow free my voice will ring out
Ac.Gtr.
Gtr.

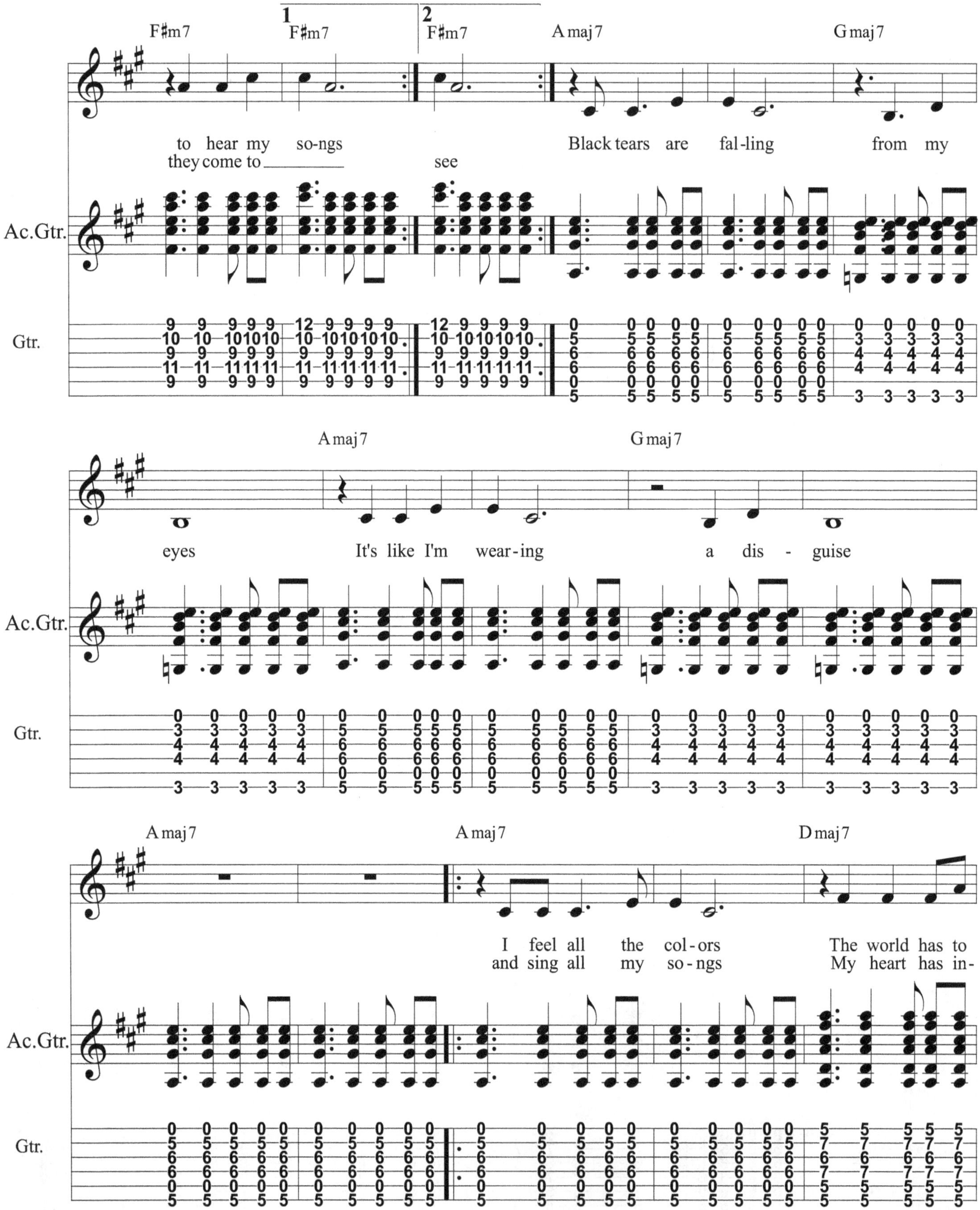
F♯m7
1 F♯m7
2 F♯m7
A maj7
G maj7
to hear my so-ngs
they come to see
Black tears are fal-ling from my
Ac.Gtr.
Gtr.
A maj7
G maj7
eyes It's like I'm wear-ing a dis - guise
Ac.Gtr.
Gtr.
A maj7
A maj7
D maj7
I feel all the col-ors The world has to
and sing all my so-ngs My heart has in-
Ac.Gtr.
Gtr.

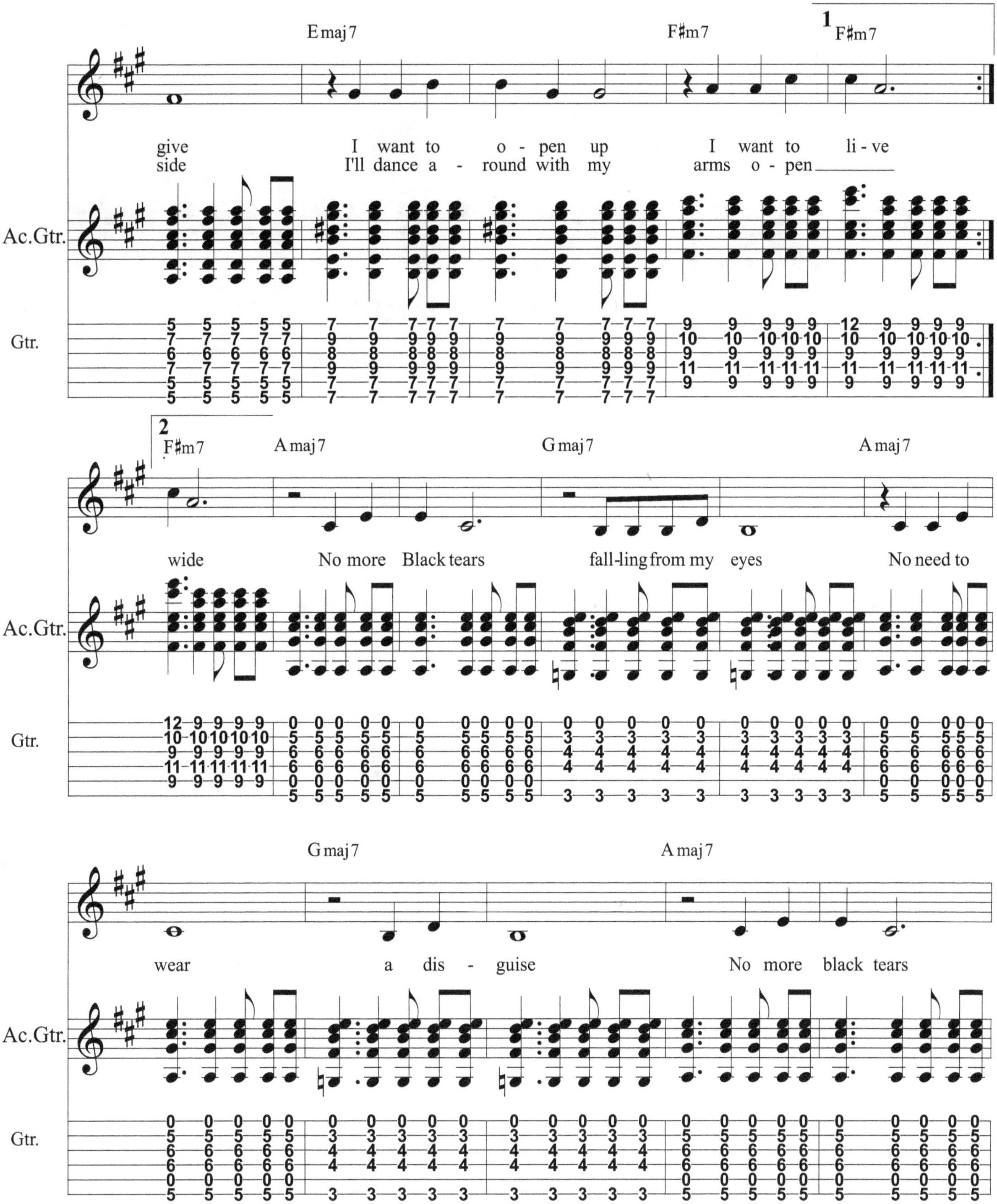
Emaj7
F♯m7
1 F♯m7
give I want to o - pen up I want to li - ve
side I'll dance a - round with my arms o - pen
Ac.Gtr.
Gtr.
2 F♯m7
Amaj7
Gmaj7
Amaj7
wide No more Black tears fall-ling from my eyes No need to
Ac.Gtr.
Gtr.
Gmaj7
Amaj7
wear a dis - guise No more black tears
Ac.Gtr.
Gtr.

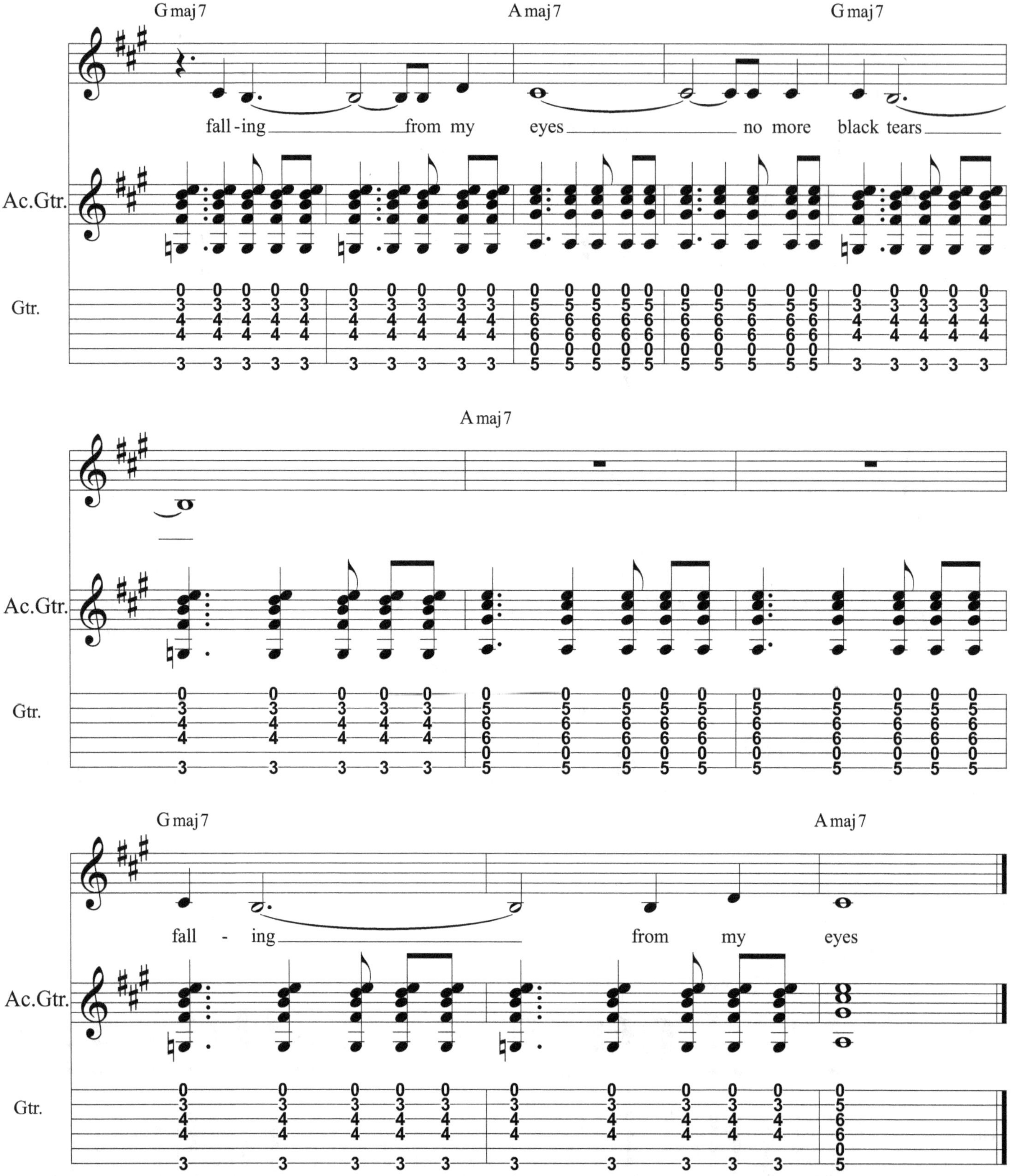
G maj 7
A maj 7
G maj 7
fall - ing from my eyes no more black tears
Ac.Gtr.
Gtr.
A maj 7
Ac.Gtr.
Gtr.
G maj 7
A maj 7
fall - ing from my eyes
Ac.Gtr.
Gtr.

# Bright Eyes

Helen Lapakko

Lyrics:

see my lit-tle daugh-ter

her eyes shin-ing so bright    I read her stor-ies and we    cud-dle at

night    She loves to    gig-gle_____ and hold my    hand

33

she loves to gig-gle cuz she feels so grand  As she ___ grows
One day she said

old - er her eyes grow dull  She seems to be
mom I'm afraid I'm gon-na die  I feel so crazy

lo - sing _____ her _ soul _____  I miss my
I don't _____ know why _____

daugh-ter _____ her eyes shin-ing so bright  I miss my daugh-ter and

cud - dling at night  I miss her gig-gles _____ and hold-ing my

34

Lyrics:

hand     I miss her gig-gles cuz she feels so grand

There was so much us-ing and an-ger in her world     I tried to reach
I saw so much pain and hurt in her eyes     I couldn't reach

in and grab hold of my lit-tle girl
in and com-fort her cries

I miss my daugh-ter her eyes shin-ing so bright     I miss my

daugh-ter and cud-dling at night     I miss her gig-gles

35

and hold-ing my hand    I miss her gig-gles    cuz    she feels so

grand    Then one day she called    and said    mom    please ___ come
The next day she left    and was    gone    twenty-eight days

and bring me    home ___ to that    place _____    I be - long _____
when I saw    her again she'd    lost that    drug ___ fill -ed    gaze _____

I've got my daugh-ter back and her eyes    shine so    bright

we love to    sit    and    talk in-to the    night    Some-times we gig-gle_____ and she holds my hand Yes, we just

gig gle cuz we feels so grand

I see my daugh ter now and her eyes shine so bright

I know her dreams will all come true to - night

37

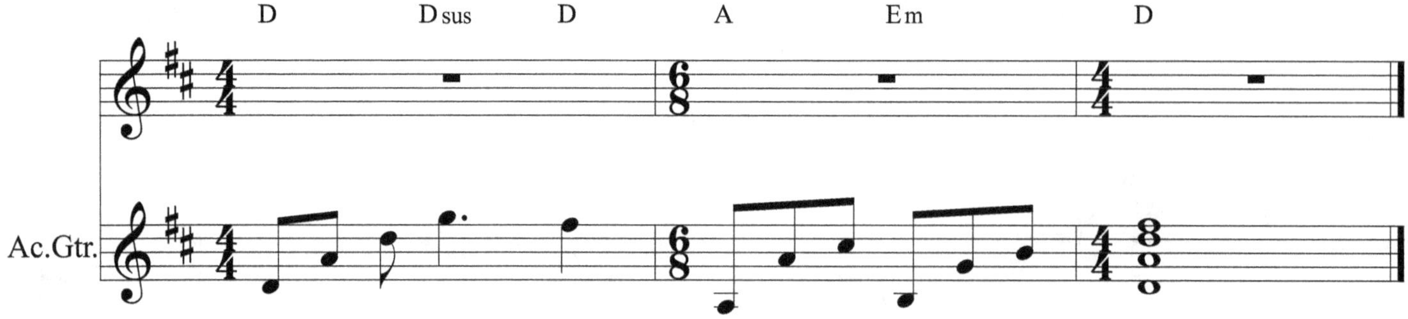
D
Dsus
D
A
Em
D
Ac.Gtr.

# Devil In My Headlights

Helen Lapakko

I was driv - in' down the street    I was    up to no good, there was a

de - vil in my head - lights    and    an - gel on my hood    It was time    to

spread my wings _____    and let my - self    sing

When I got to that bar room door it was o - pen and read - y for
I___ jumped up___ on the stage and I grab - bed___ a___ gui -

me
tat

There were no - thin' but cow - boys far as I could
The mic - ro - phone was ready so I sang to that___

see
bar

I was driv - in' down the street I was

up to no good, there was a de - vil in my head - lights and an - gel on my hood

It was time to spread my wings ____ and let my-self sing

You could-a heard a pin drop sur-prised at me
and when the song ____ end-ed there was-n't a

song The air was charged e-lec-tric ____ at what I had
sound then some-one star-ted clap-ping there was applause all a-

done
-round

I was driv-in' down the street I was

41

up to no good, there was a de - vil in my head - lights and an - gel on my hood

It was time to spread my wings_____ and let my - self sing

Then the ow-ner of the gui-tar he came and shook my
now ev-ry night you'll find me_____ sing-ing in some

hand He said you know we're look-ing for a sing-er in our
bar the name it does-n't mat-ter I just call it the wish-ing

band
star

I was driv-in' down the street I was

up to no good, there was a de-vil in my head-lights and an-gel on my hood

43

It was time to spread my wings _____ and let my-self sing

I was driv-in' down the street I was up to no good, there was a

de - vil in my head-lights and an-gel on my hood It was time to

spread my wings _____ and let my-self sing and let my-self

sing                    and let my-self    sing

# Disconnected Lives

Helen Lapakko

Voice

Acoustic Guitar

Gtr.

I'm from an i vory tow - er of
fa - ther was a hus - tler his

dis - con - nec - ted lives Where whis - key makes a ri - ver of so — man-y
mo-ther walked the streets ___ He knew how to love me and he knew how to

46

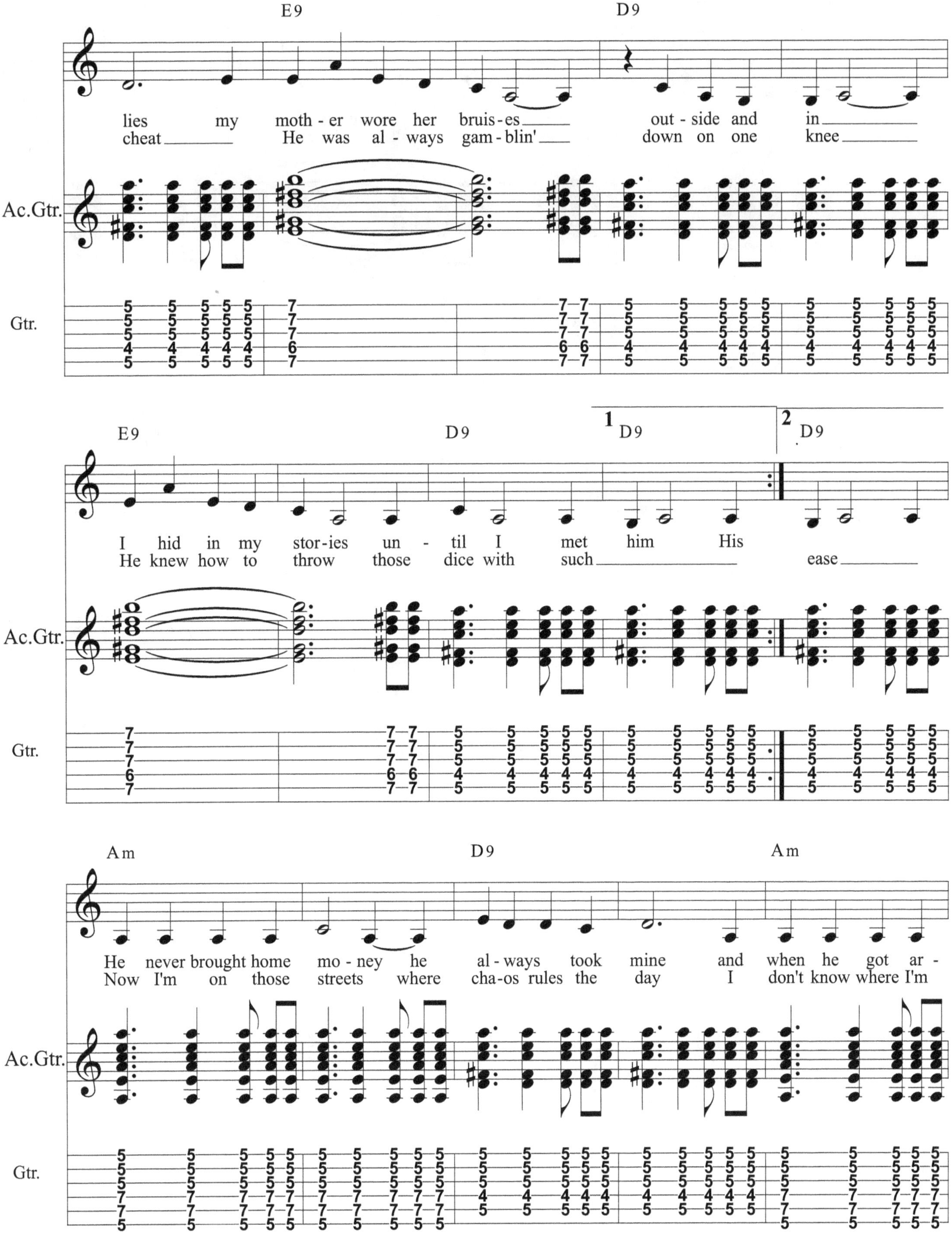
E9
D9
lies my moth - er wore her bruis - es out - side and in
cheat He was al - ways gam - blin' down on one knee
Ac.Gtr.
Gtr.
E9
D9
1 D9
2 D9
I hid in my stor - ies un - til I met him His
He knew how to throw those dice with such ease
Ac.Gtr.
Gtr.
Am
D9
Am
He never brought home mo - ney he al - ways took mine and when he got ar -
Now I'm on those streets where cha - os rules the day I don't know where I'm
Ac.Gtr.
Gtr.

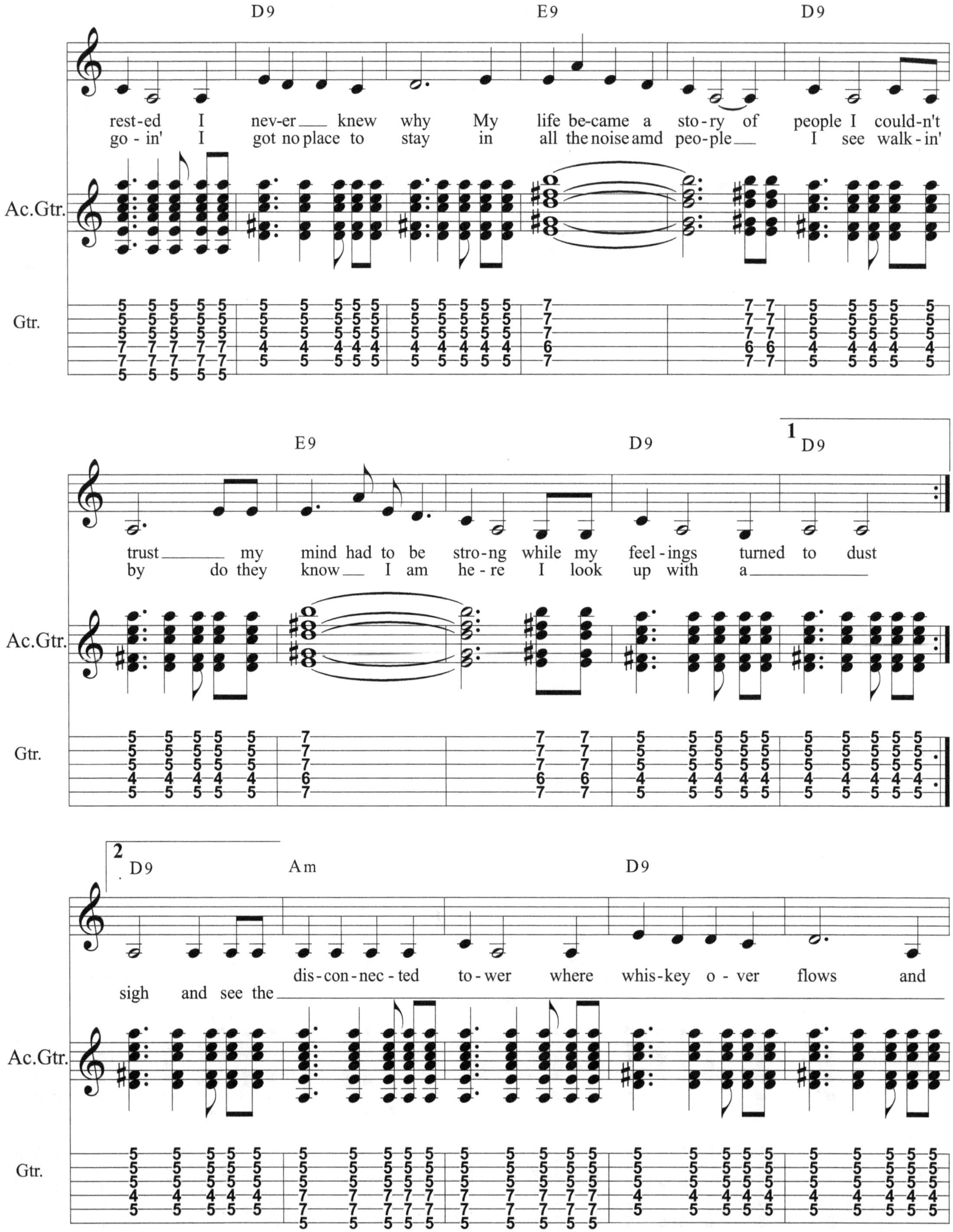
D9 E9 D9
rest-ed I nev-er knew why My life be-came a sto-ry of people I could-n't
go - in' I got no place to stay in all the noise amd peo-ple I see walk-in'
Ac.Gtr.
Gtr.
E9 D9 1 D9
trust my mind had to be stro-ng while my feel-ings turned to dust
by do they know I am he-re I look up with a
Ac.Gtr.
Gtr.
2 D9 Am D9
dis-con-nec-ted to-wer where whis-key o-ver flows and
sigh and see the
Ac.Gtr.
Gtr.

no one stops and sees the bruis - es from the blows

They're not on the out-side They hide deep with - in___ I'm the one who

sees them cuz I know where I've been___

from an i-vory tow-er of dis-con-nec-ted lives where whis-key makes a

I'm

51

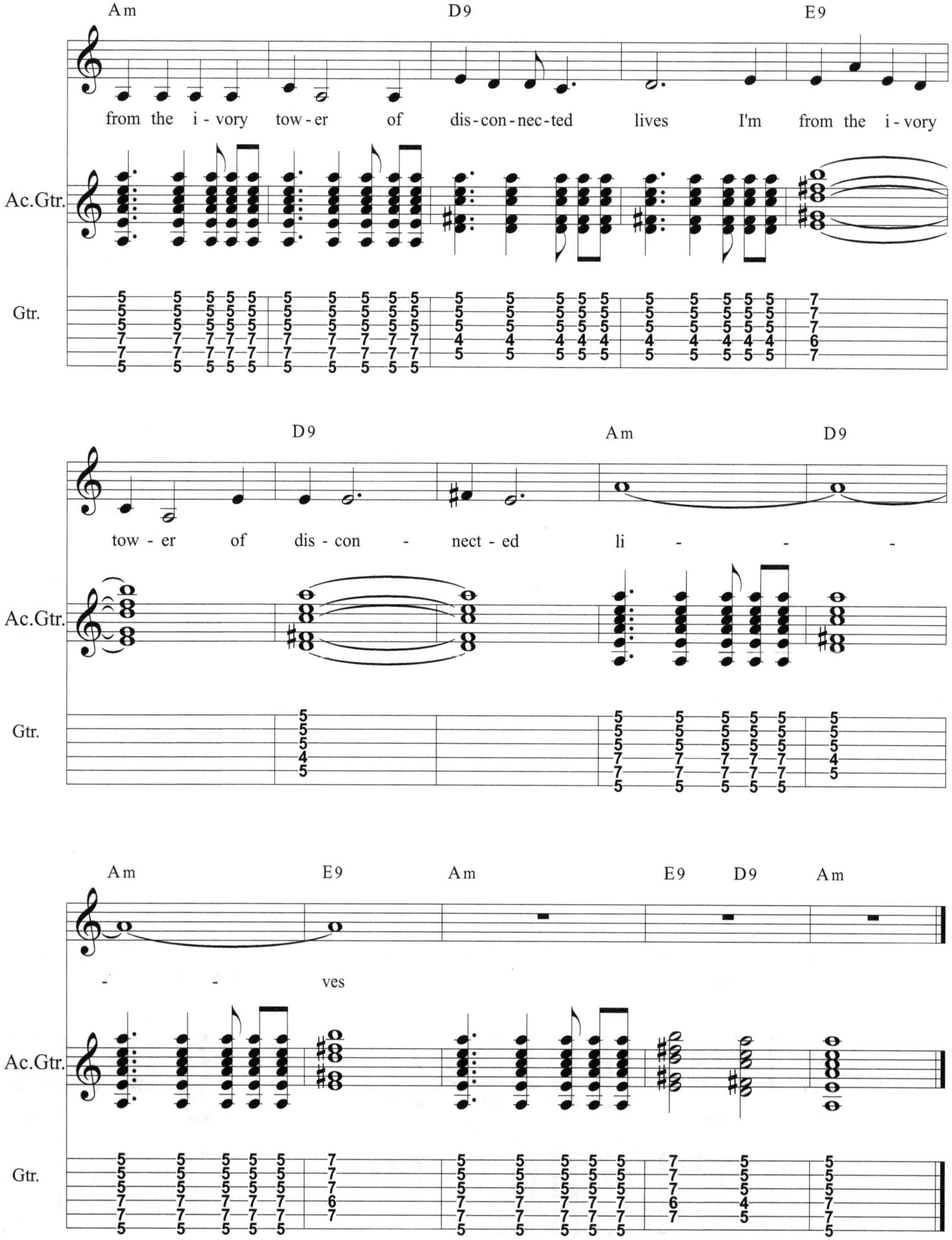
Am
D9
E9
from the i - vory tow - er of dis - con - nec - ted lives I'm from the i - vory
Ac.Gtr.
Gtr.
D9
Am
D9
tow - er of dis - con - nect - ed li - - - - -
Ac.Gtr.
Gtr.
Am
E9
Am
E9
D9
Am
- - ves
Ac.Gtr.
Gtr.

# Finding My Way Back Home

Helen Lapakko

Lyrics:

I look in -
It ___ is

side
such

and see those fa - ces
a hard path to fol - low

and parts of me I left be -
when you're ___ lost and so

hind ___
sca - red

a lit - tle girl
I used to feel

with eyes full of
the spir - it ___

53

won-der ... a - noth-er who's sad ... and so a - fraid
in me ... It would guide me ... on___ my way

No one was there ... to see her beau-ty
My legs feel heavy ... My arms are ti-red

no one was there to hold her hand ... She lived in a
hands emp - ty no - where to go___ ... now___ that

world ... of i - mag - i - na - tion ... cre - a - ting peo-ple who would
voice ... is qui - et in - side me ... and I can't hear___ those

54

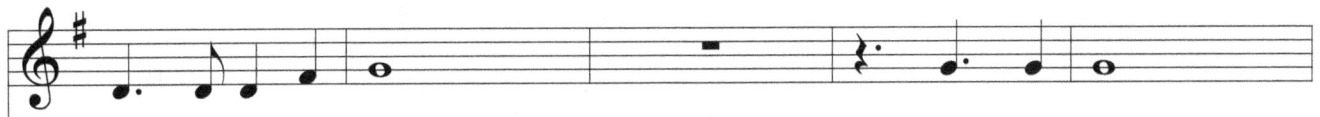

love    and un - der - stand
guid -       ing words                    All    a - lone

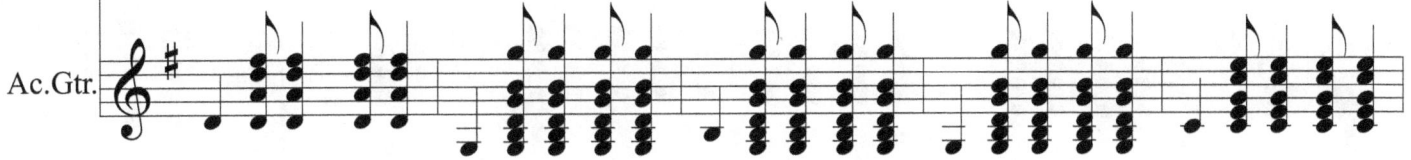

on    this  jour - ney_____    Trying  to  find   my  way  home

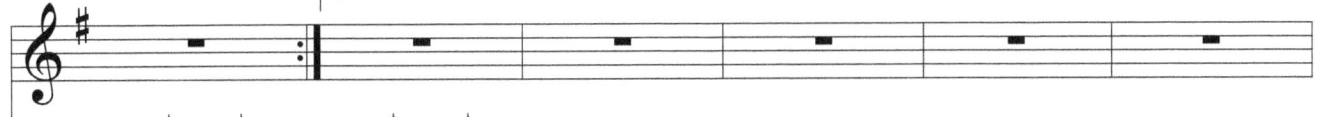

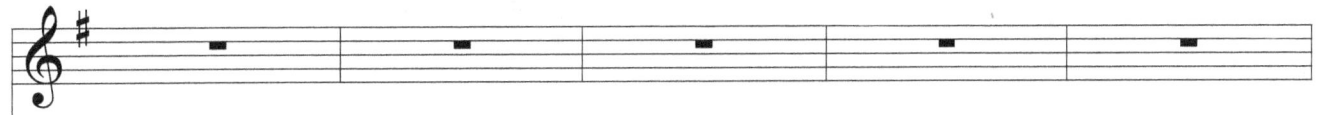

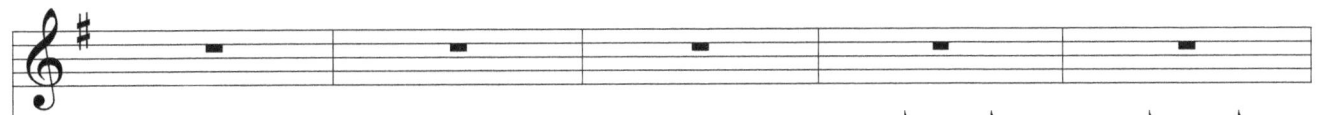

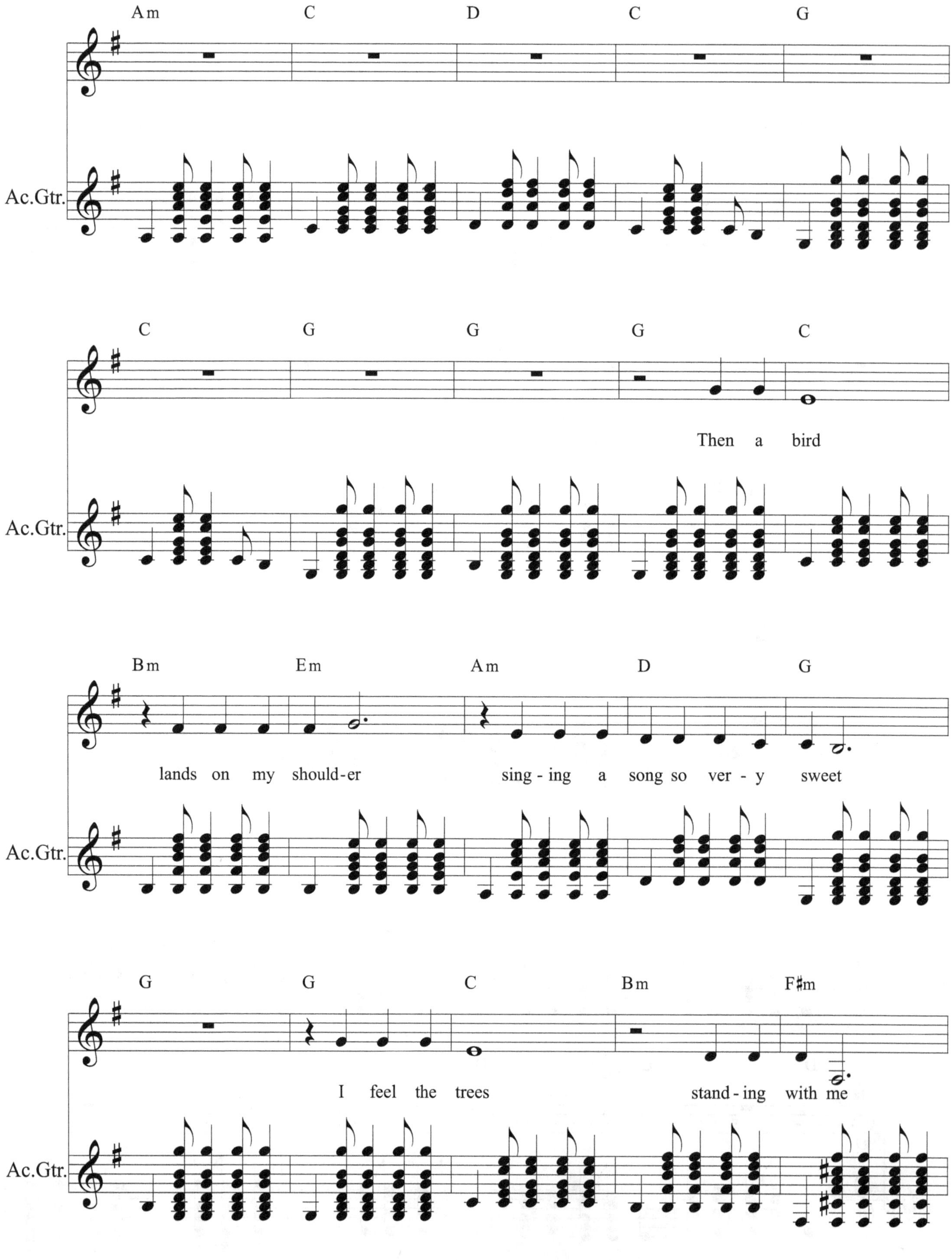

Am C D C G
Ac.Gtr.
C G G G C
Then a bird
Ac.Gtr.
Bm Em Am D G
lands on my shoulder-er singing - ing a song so ver - y sweet
Ac.Gtr.
G G C Bm F♯m
I feel the trees stand - ing with me
Ac.Gtr.

blow - ing soft - ly      a gen - tle breeze

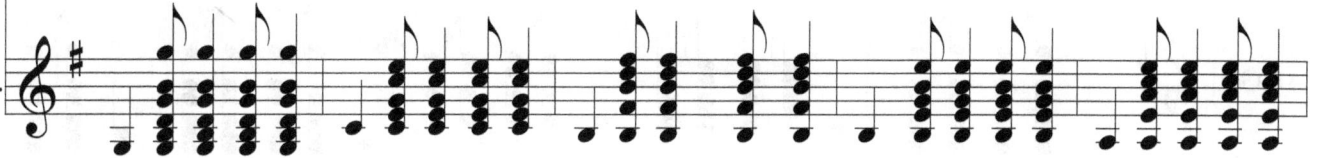

The sun is warm      it com-forts my bo - dy      I can

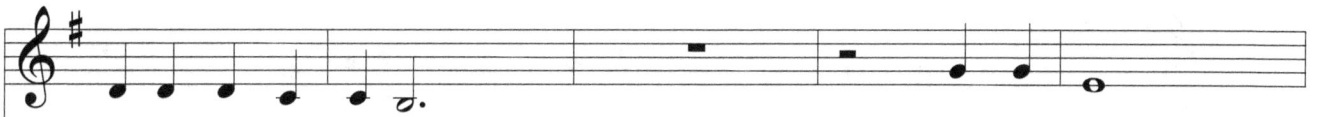

feel its heal - ing rays___      Here I stand

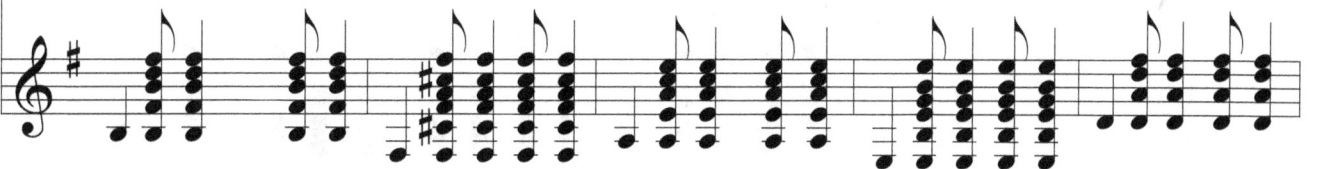

in the beau-ty of na-ture      feel-ing the touch      of God's own

G G G C D
hand Not a lone on this
Ac.Gtr.
G C D G G
jour ney___ Trying to find my way home
Ac.Gtr.
G C D G C
I'm not a - lone on this jour ney___ Trying to
Ac.Gtr.
D G G G C
find my way home trying to
Ac.Gtr.

find               my way  ho - me

# Got to Keep on Going

Helen Lapakko

Got to_____ keep on_____

go - in'_____ Got to_____ keep on_____ grow - in'_____

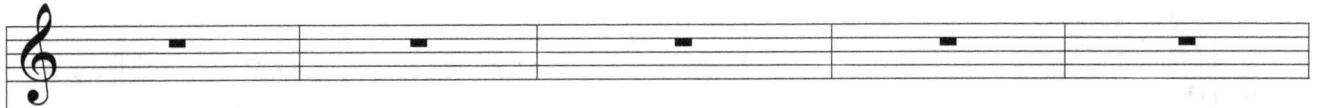
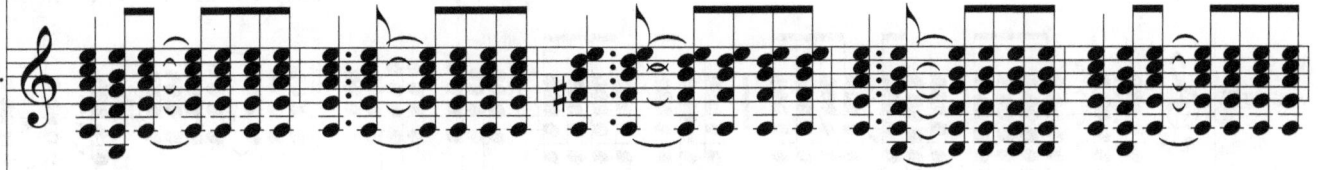
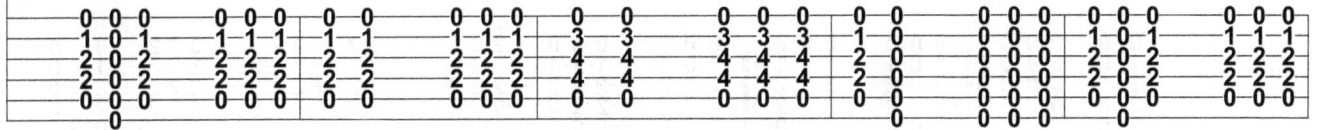

My head is filled with a____ smok - y haze I can't
The words come out_____ but noone hears I'm a -

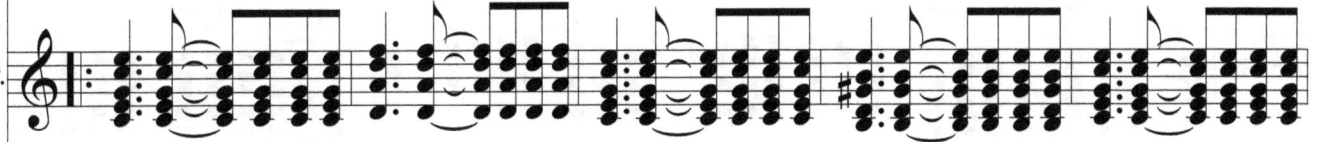
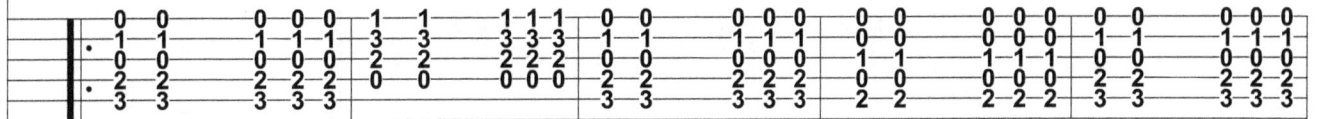

see I'm to in a da -      -      -      -      -
lone to shed my tear -     -      -      -      -

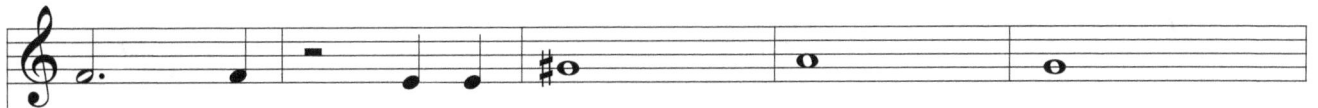
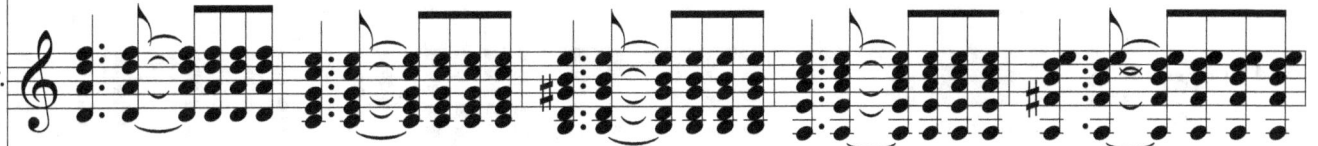
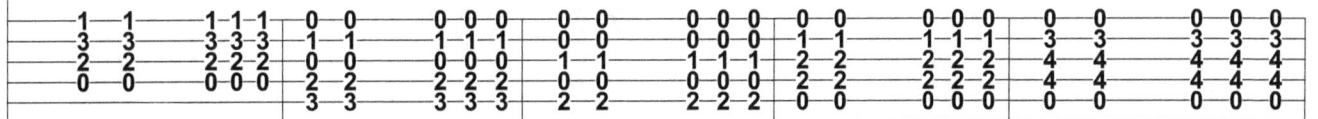

61

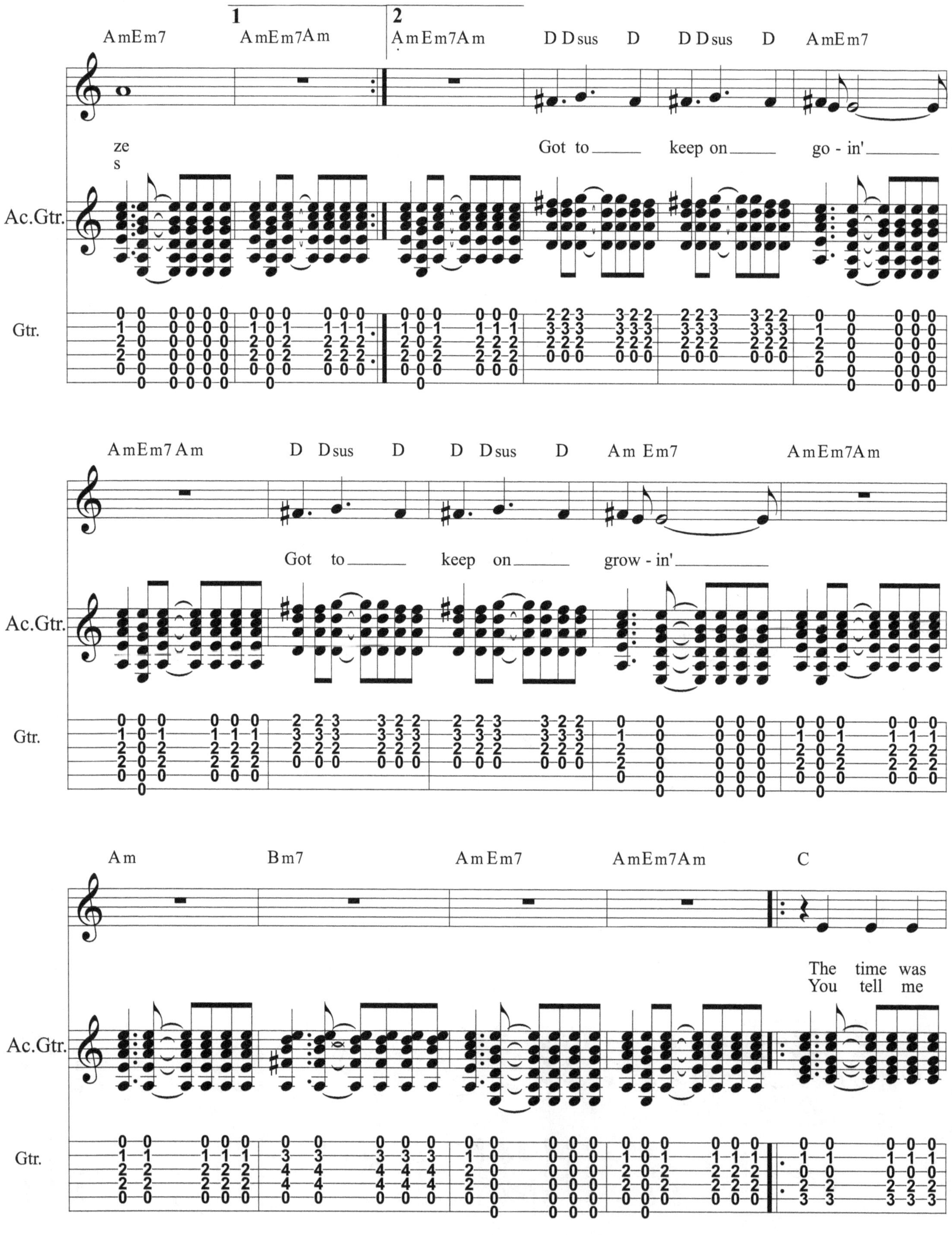
AmEm7
1
AmEm7Am
2
AmEm7Am
D Dsus D D Dsus D AmEm7
ze
s
Got to keep on go - in'
Ac.Gtr.
Gtr.
AmEm7Am
D Dsus D D Dsus D Am Em7 AmEm7Am
Got to keep on grow - in'
Ac.Gtr.
Gtr.
Am Bm7 AmEm7 AmEm7Am C
The time was
You tell me
Ac.Gtr.
Gtr.

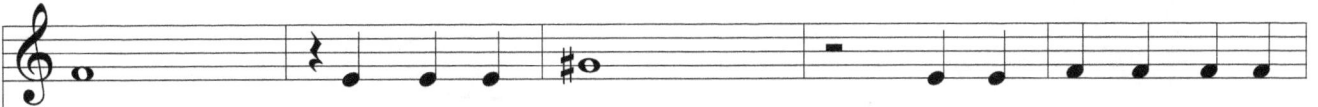

dark

stories

There was no light

I fall in deep

Then I met you on that

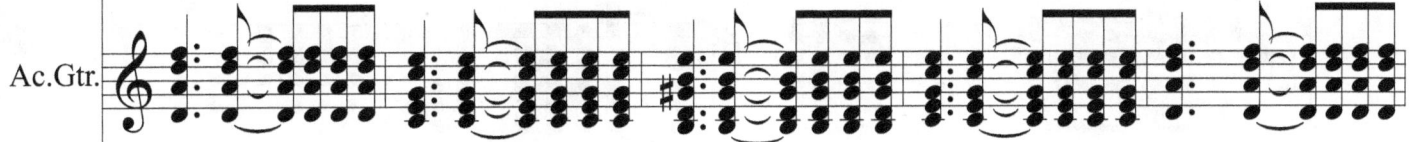

```
Gtr.
1   1       1 1 1     0   0      0 0 0     0   0      0 0 0     0   0      0 0 0     1   1      1 1 1
3   3       3 3 3     1   1      1 1 1     0   0      0 0 0     1   1      1 1 1     3   3      3 3 3
2   2       2 2 2     0   0      0 0 0     1   1      1 1 1     0   0      0 0 0     2   2      2 2 2
0   0       0 0 0     2   2      2 2 2     0   0      0 0 0     0   2      2 2 2     0   0      0 0 0
                      3   3      3 3 3     2   2      2 2 2     3   3      3 3 3
```

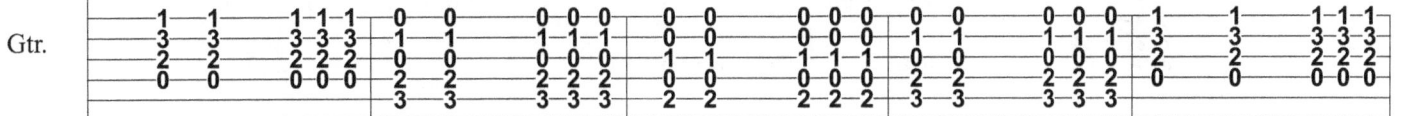

fate - ful ni - - - - - ght

I can't sle - - - - - ep

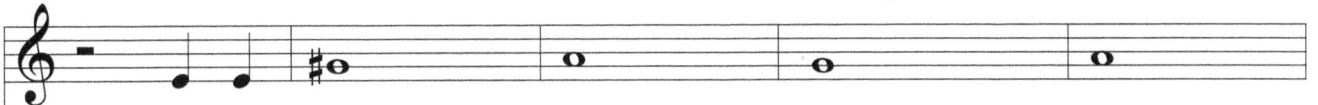

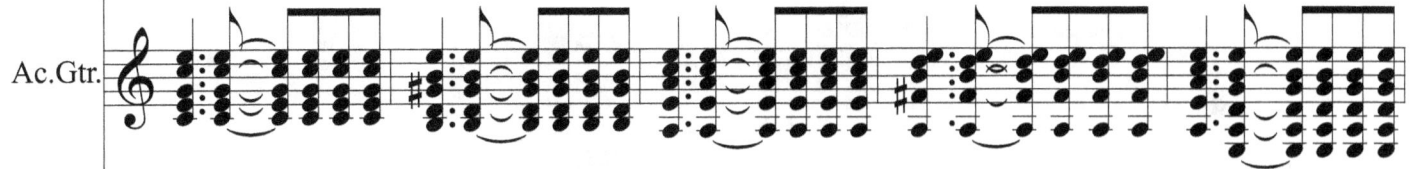

```
Gtr.
0   0       0 0 0     0   0      0 0 0     0   0      0 0 0     0   0      0 0 0     0   0      0 0 0 0
1   1       1 1 1     0   0      0 0 0     1   1      1 1 1     3   3      3 3 3     1   0      0 0 0 0
0   0       0 0 0     1   1      1 1 1     2   2      2 2 2     4   4      4 4 4     2   0      0 0 0 0
2   2       2 2 2     0   0      0 0 0     2   2      2 2 2     4   4      4 4 4     2   0      0 0 0 0
3   3       3 3 3     2   2      2 2 2     0   0      0 0 0     0   0      0 0 0     0   0      0 0 0 0
                                                                                               0   0      0 0 0 0
```

**1** AmEm7Am   **2** AmEm7Am   D Dsus   D   DDsus   D   AmEm7   AmEm7Am

Got to _____ keep on _____ go - in' _____

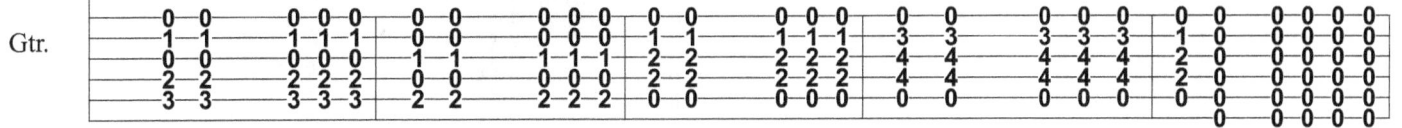

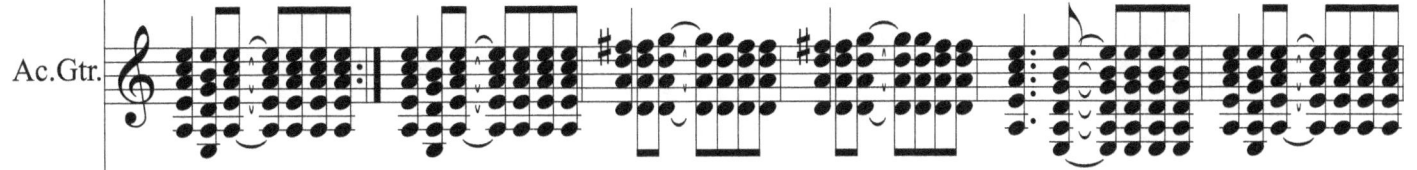

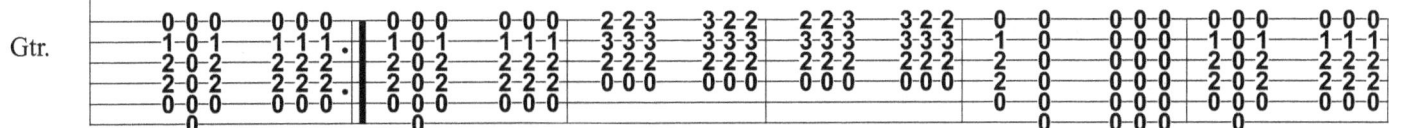

```
Gtr.
0 0 0   0 0 0     0 0 0   0 0 0     2 2 3   3 2 2     2 2 3   3 2 2     0   0      0 0 0     0 0 0   0 0 0
1 0 1   1 1 1     1 0 1   1 1 1     3 3 3   3 3 3     3 3 3   3 3 3     1   0      0 0 0     1 0 1   1 1 1
2 0 2   2 2 2     2 0 2   2 2 2     0 0 0   0 0 0     0 0 0   0 0 0     2   0      0 0 0     2 0 2   2 2 2
2 0 2   2 2 2     2 0 2   2 2 2     0 0 0   0 0 0     0 0 0   0 0 0     2   0      0 0 0     2 0 2   2 2 2
0 0 0   0 0 0     0 0 0   0 0 0                                        0   0      0 0 0     0 0 0   0 0 0
0                 0                                                                          0
```

63

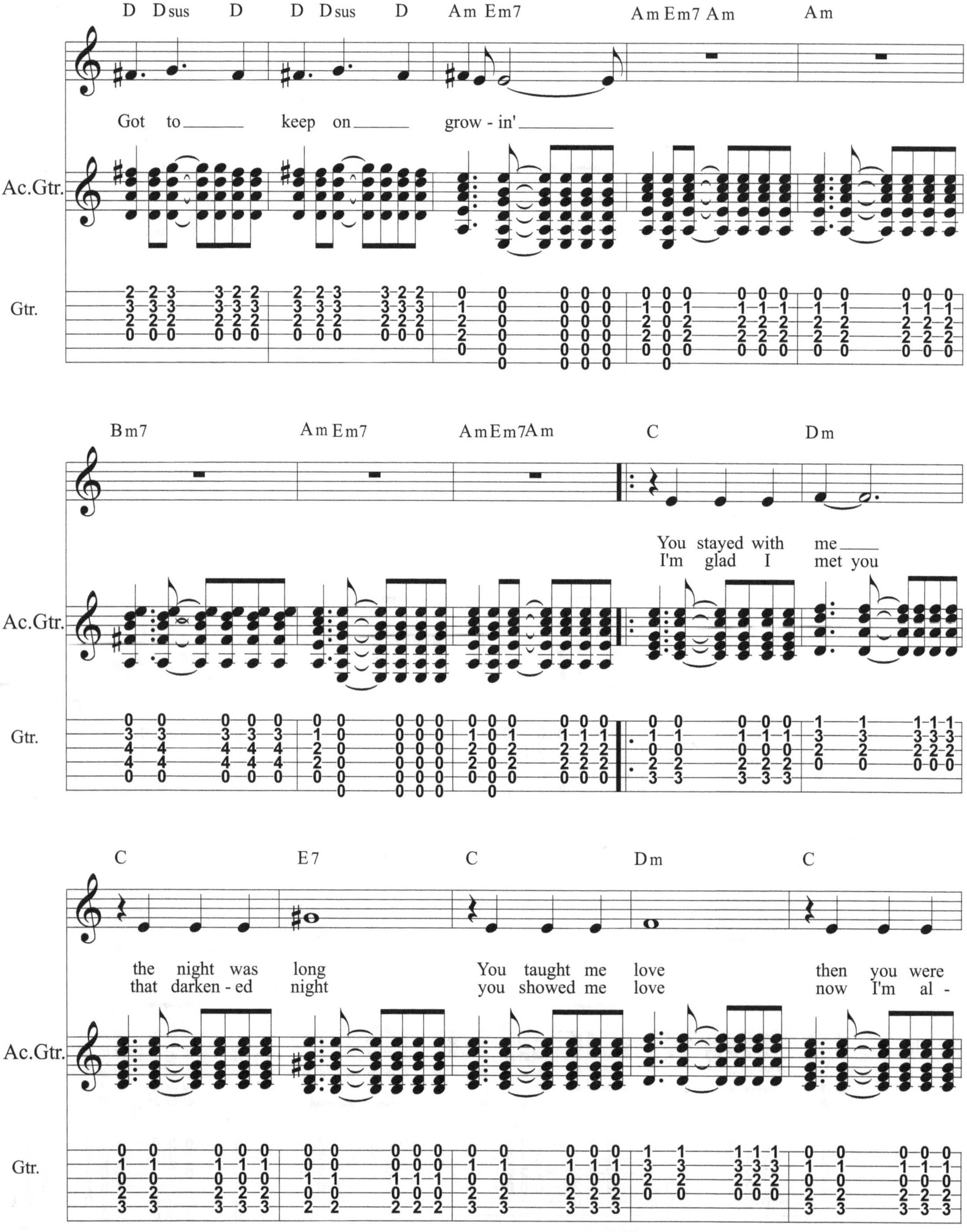
D Dsus D D Dsus D Am Em7 Am Em7 Am Am
Got to keep on grow - in'
Ac.Gtr.
Gtr.
Bm7 Am Em7 Am Em7 Am C Dm
You stayed with me
I'm glad I met you
Ac.Gtr.
Gtr.
C E7 C Dm C
the night was long
that darken - ed night
You taught me love
you showed me love
then you were
now I'm al -
Ac.Gtr.
Gtr.

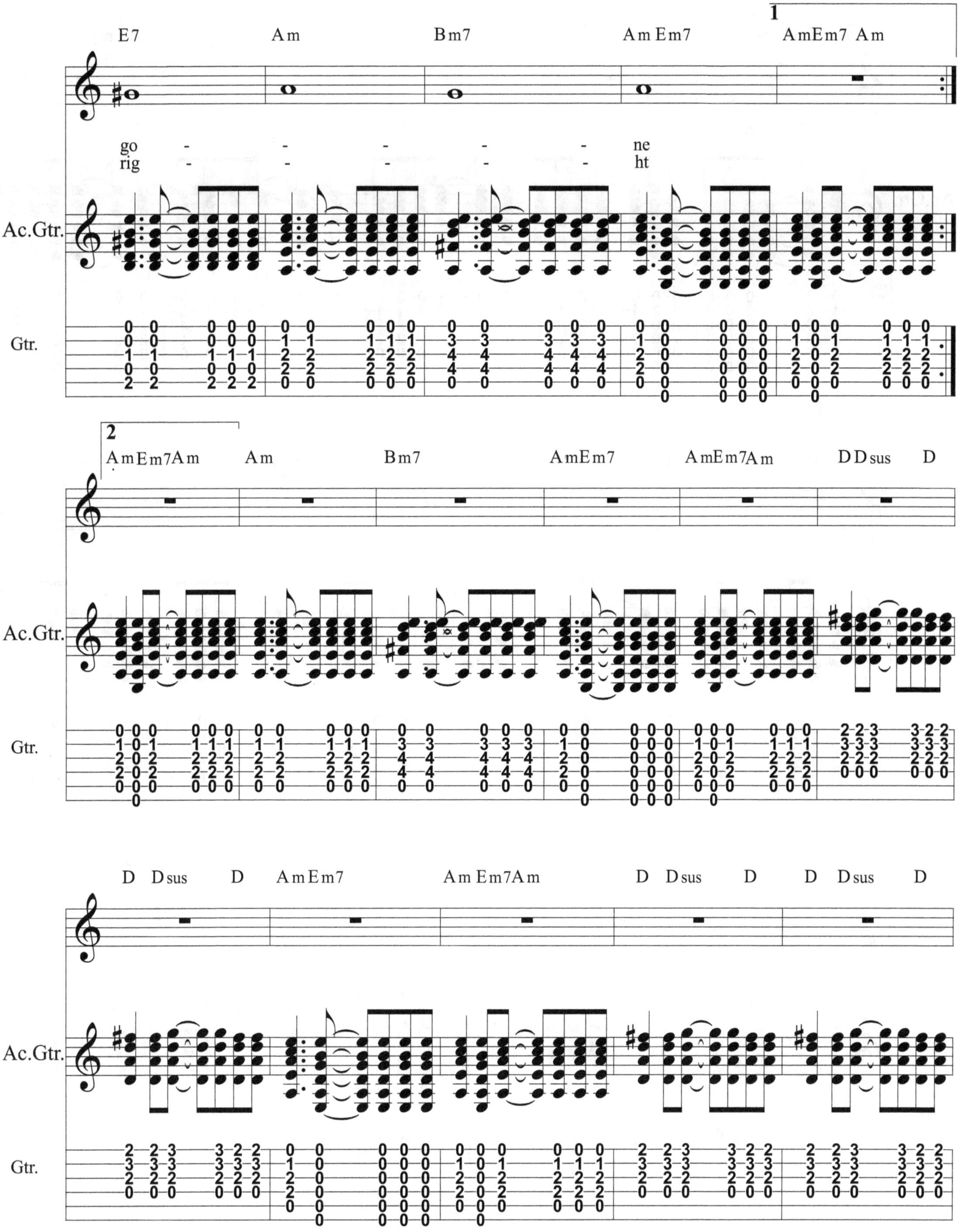
1
E7
Am
Bm7
AmEm7
AmEm7 Am
go - - - - - ne
rig - - - - - ht
Ac.Gtr.
Gtr.
2
AmEm7Am
Am
Bm7
AmEm7
AmEm7Am
D Dsus D
Ac.Gtr.
Gtr.
D Dsus D
AmEm7
Am Em7Am
D Dsus D
D Dsus D
Ac.Gtr.
Gtr.

Chords: Am Em7 · Am Em7 Am · Am · Bm7 · Am Em7

Am Em7 Am · Am · Bm7 · Am Em7 · Am Em7 Am

C · F · G · Am · C

I was weak and you were stro-ng You helped me

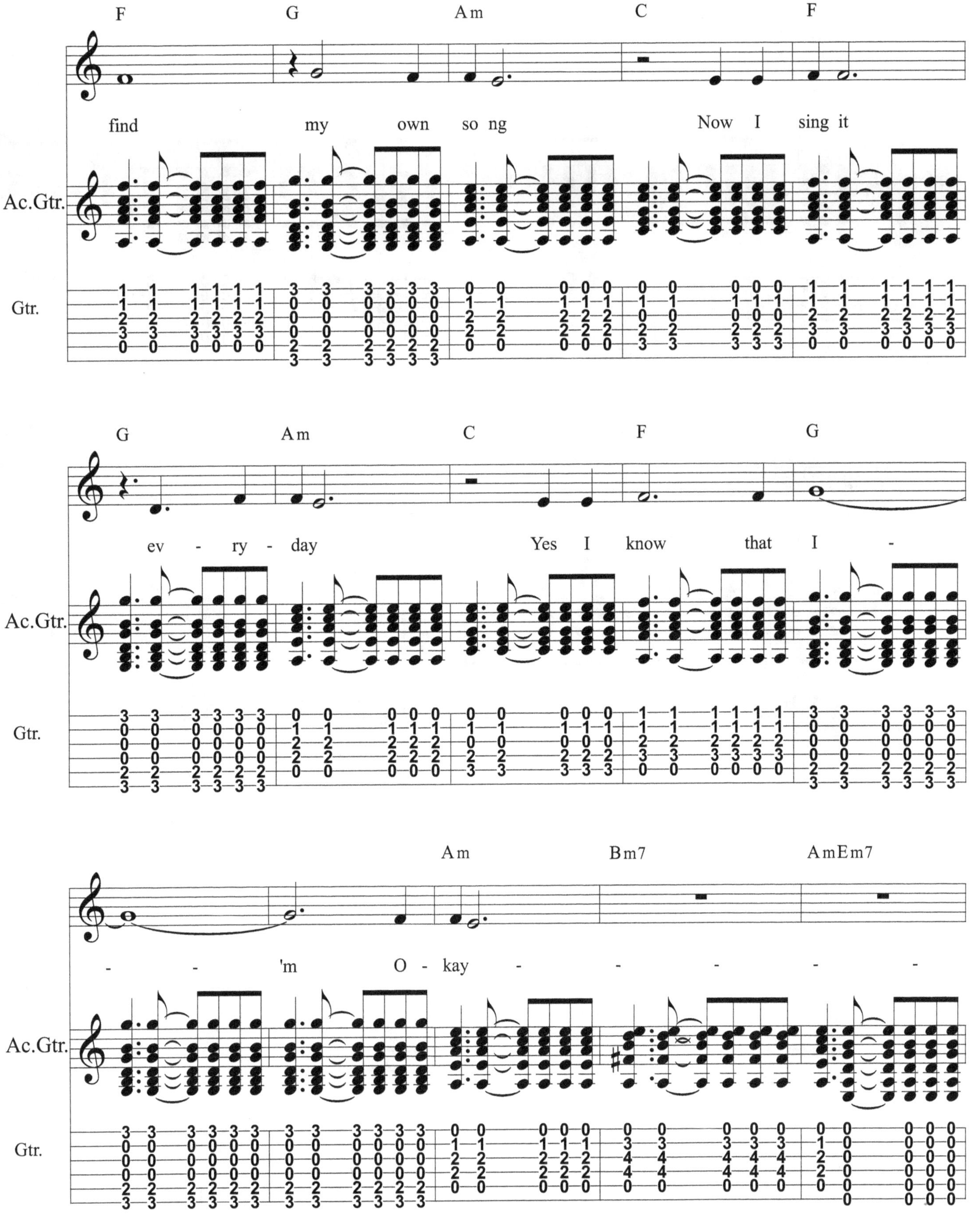
F G Am C F
find my own so ng Now I sing it
Ac.Gtr.
Gtr.
G Am C F G
ev - ry - day Yes I know that I -
Ac.Gtr.
Gtr.
Am Bm7 AmEm7
- - 'm O - kay - - - - -
Ac.Gtr.
Gtr.

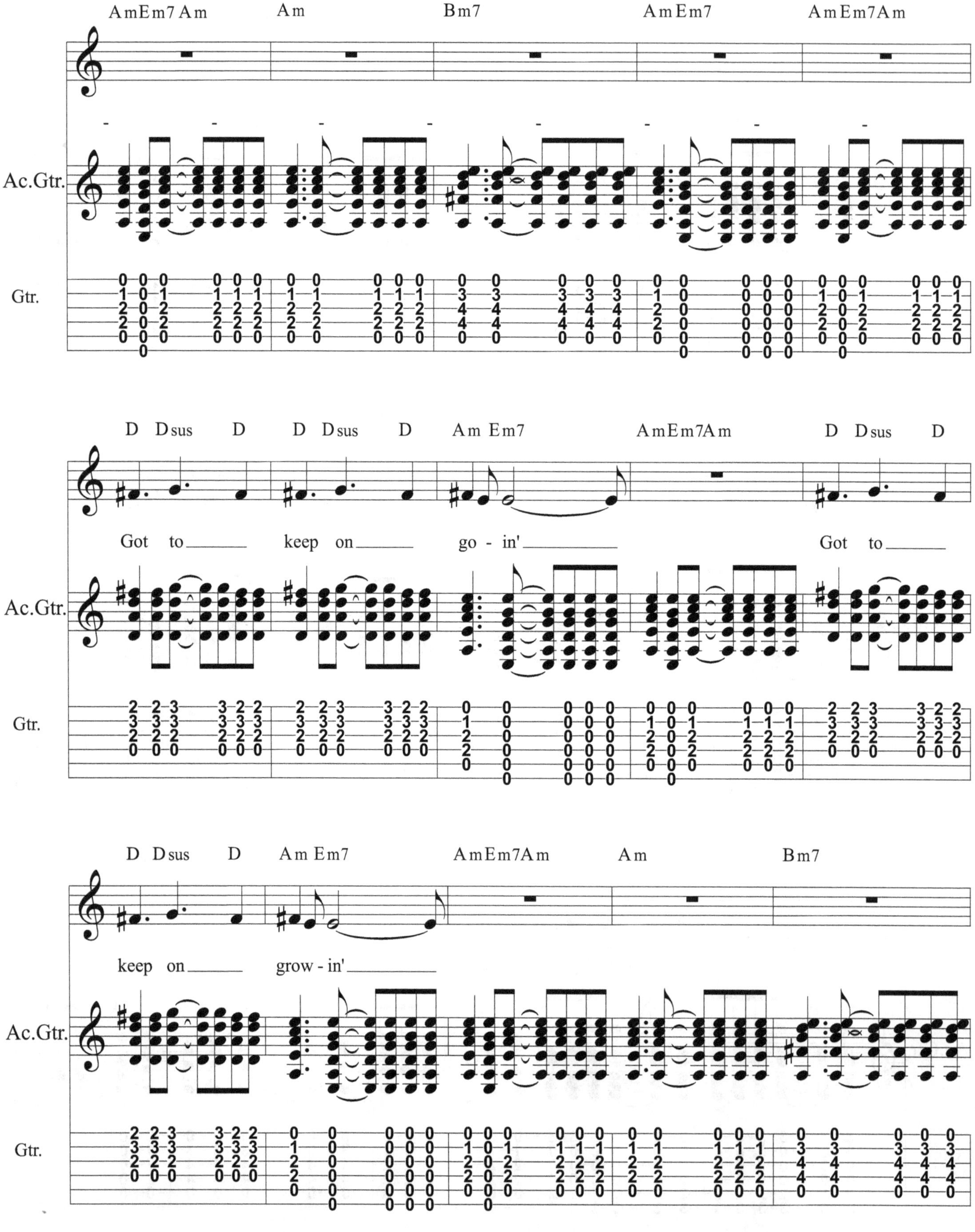
AmEm7 Am
Am
Bm7
AmEm7
AmEm7Am
Ac.Gtr.
Gtr.
D Dsus D
D Dsus D
Am Em7
AmEm7Am
D Dsus D
Got to keep on go - in' Got to
Ac.Gtr.
Gtr.
D Dsus D
Am Em7
AmEm7Am
Am
Bm7
keep on grow - in'
Ac.Gtr.
Gtr.

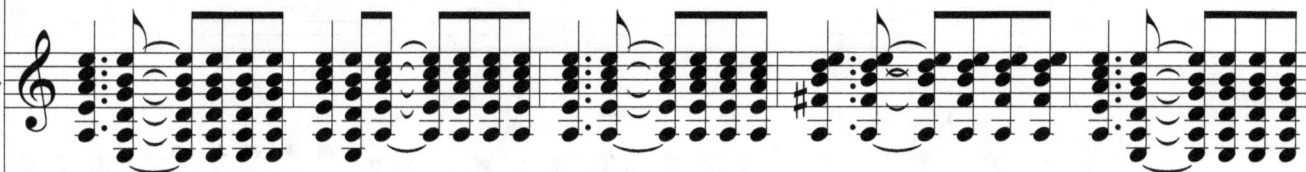

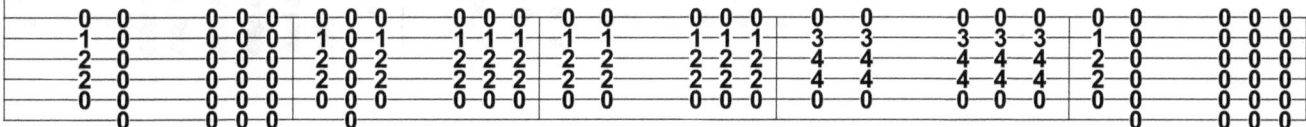

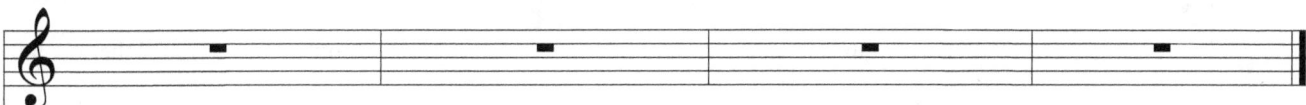

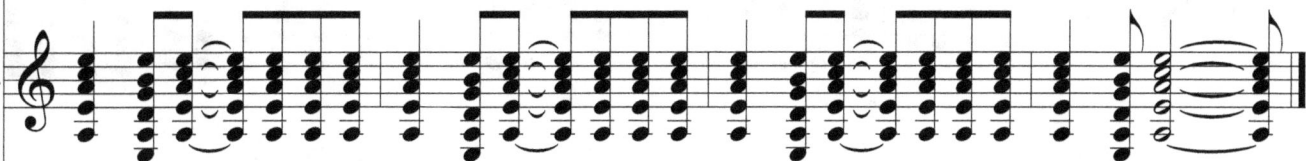

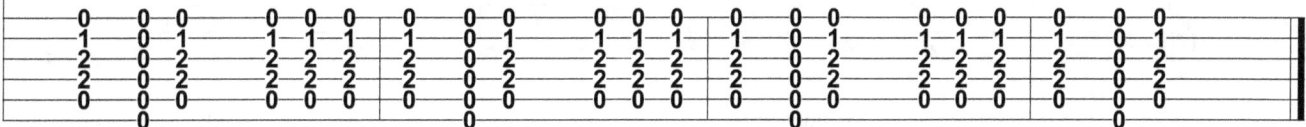

69

# Guitar Man

Helen Lapakko

Oh gui-tar man _____ sit-tin' o - ver there _____ gui-

tar nes - tled in your arms like a ba - by _____ oh gui-tar man _____

Head full of dreams heart full of pain
Foot-ball and baseball par - ties and girlfriends

70

eyes o - pen wide        wait - ing _____        wait - ing for the
oh they pull you         here and there _____    al - ways you come

time                     when your dreams will come true _____ now _____ Oh
back                     grab your guitar that you hold so dear _____

gui-tar man _____      sit-tin' o - ver there _____ gui - tar nes-tled
gui-tar man _____

in your arms like a ba - by _____ oh gui-tar man _____

Lyrics line 1 (with chords C F G C F G C F):
pas-sion in your soul____ mu-sic in your heart please teach to

Lyrics line 2:
fing-ers____ en - twined in the strings of your life let the mu-sic

Second system (chords G D Dsus D C G):
me all that your fin-gers know_____ eyes smi-ling bright

flow way down in - si-de you_____ then play for me

Third system (chords C G D Dsus D A):
See that ear-ring glisten-ing in your ear_____ oh gui-tar man_____

play me songs you know I want to hear_____ oh, gui-tar man_____

Fourth system (1. A, 2. A, A G A):
____ sit-tin' o - ver there_____ gui-tar nes-tled

____

in your arms like a ba - by_____ oh gui-tar man_____

Pull me in close    bring me home to-night    sing me all your sto-ries

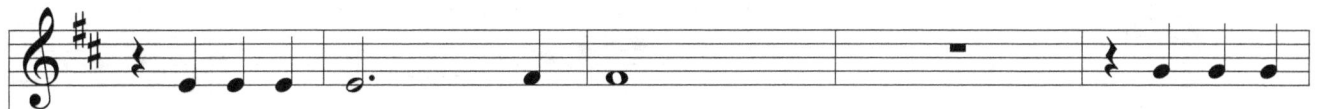

and let me stay    a - while    Share all your

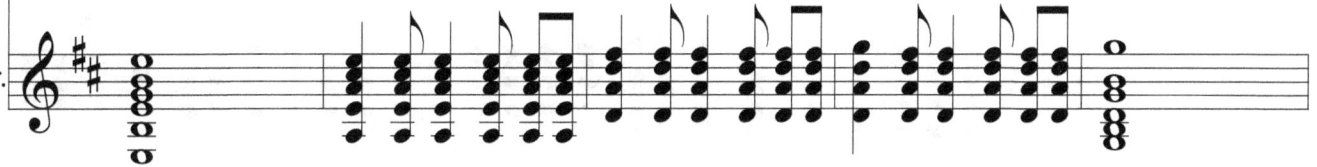

dreams    then hold me tight    lay me on the floor    and

Em F G D
we'll make love to - ni - - - ght
Ac.Gtr.
Dsus D A G
Oh gui-tar man sit-tin' o - ver there gui-
Ac.Gtr.
A G D Dsus D A
tar nes - tled in your arms like a ba - by oh gui-tar man
Ac.Gtr.
D Dsus D A
Oh gui-tar man
Ac.Gtr.

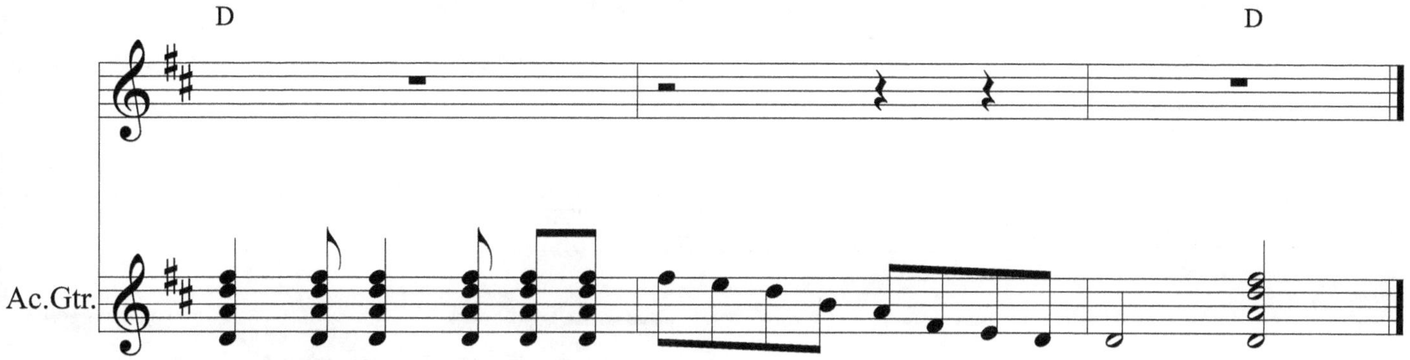
D
D
Ac.Gtr.

# I Have This Place

Helen Lapakko

I have this place so deep in-
At times this place place it hurts so

side Where at times I run and I
deep I at have trou - ble fall - ing a -

Am     Dm     Dm     Am

hide     a place I shed     my qui - et
sleep     words___ they crowd     in_____ my

Ac.Gtr.

Am     E     E     Am

tears     and try to com - fort     all     my
mind     no comfort is there that     I     can

Ac.Gtr.

Am     F     G♯m     Am

fears     ah     ah     ah
find     ah     ah     ah

Ac.Gtr.

Am     F     G♯m     Am

ah     ah     ah ah ah ah
ah     ah     ah ah ah ah

Ac.Gtr.

77

Lyrics:

I lay here my eyes are o - pen wide an - ger is boil - ing deep in - side the words are stuck no where to go my feelings are caught in - side the

78

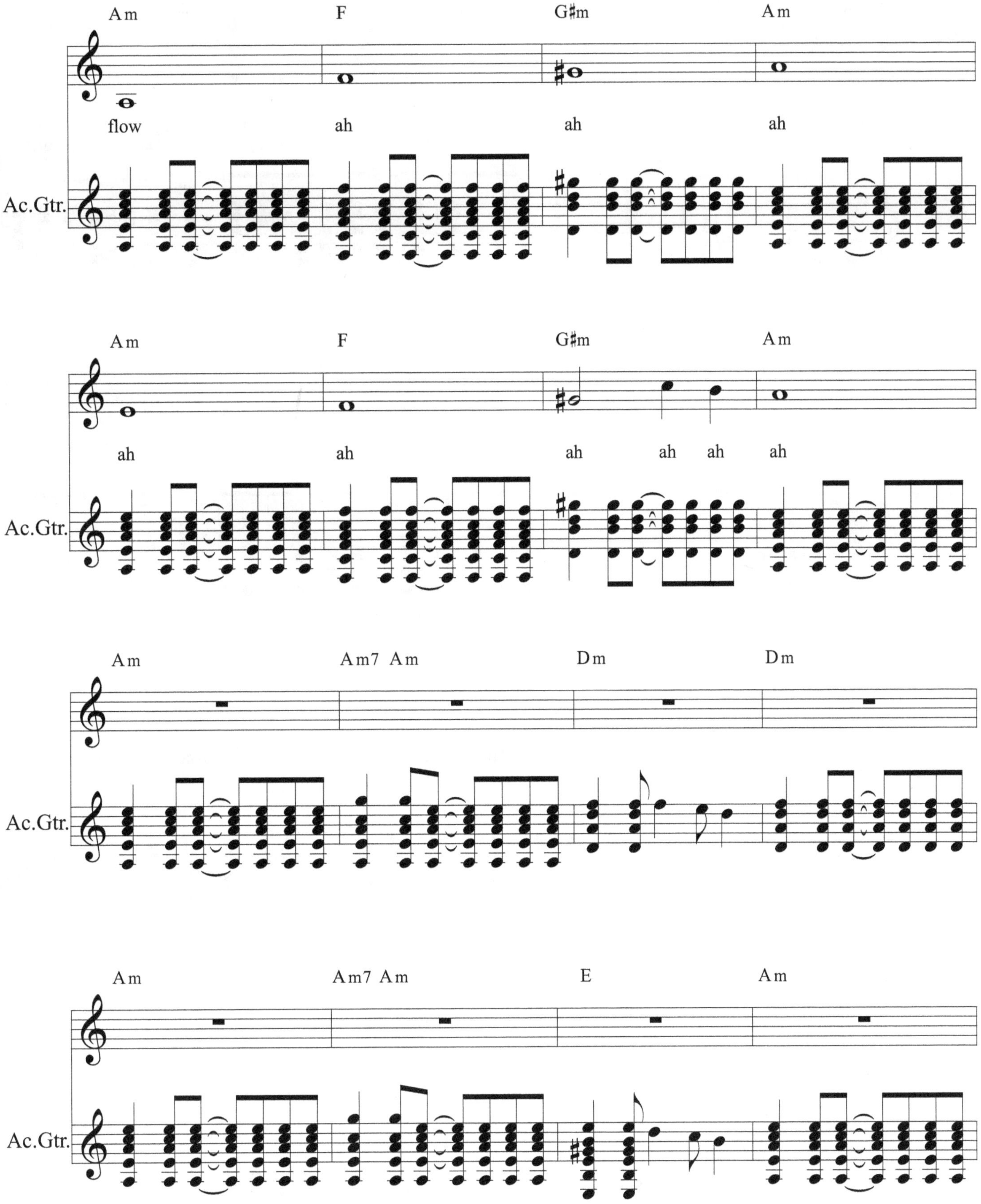
Am F G♯m Am
flow ah ah ah
Ac.Gtr.
Am F G♯m Am
ah ah ah ah ah ah
Ac.Gtr.
Am Am7 Am Dm Dm
Ac.Gtr.
Am Am7 Am E Am
Ac.Gtr.

I want to cry but my eyes stay
I know and feel things others don't

dry my mouth it o - pens out comes a
see I try to find words to set me

sigh I'm lost I'm trou - bled no com - fort in
free The ___ words flow out on ___ deaf

sight I close my eyes real hard I
ears a - gain I talk but no - one

80

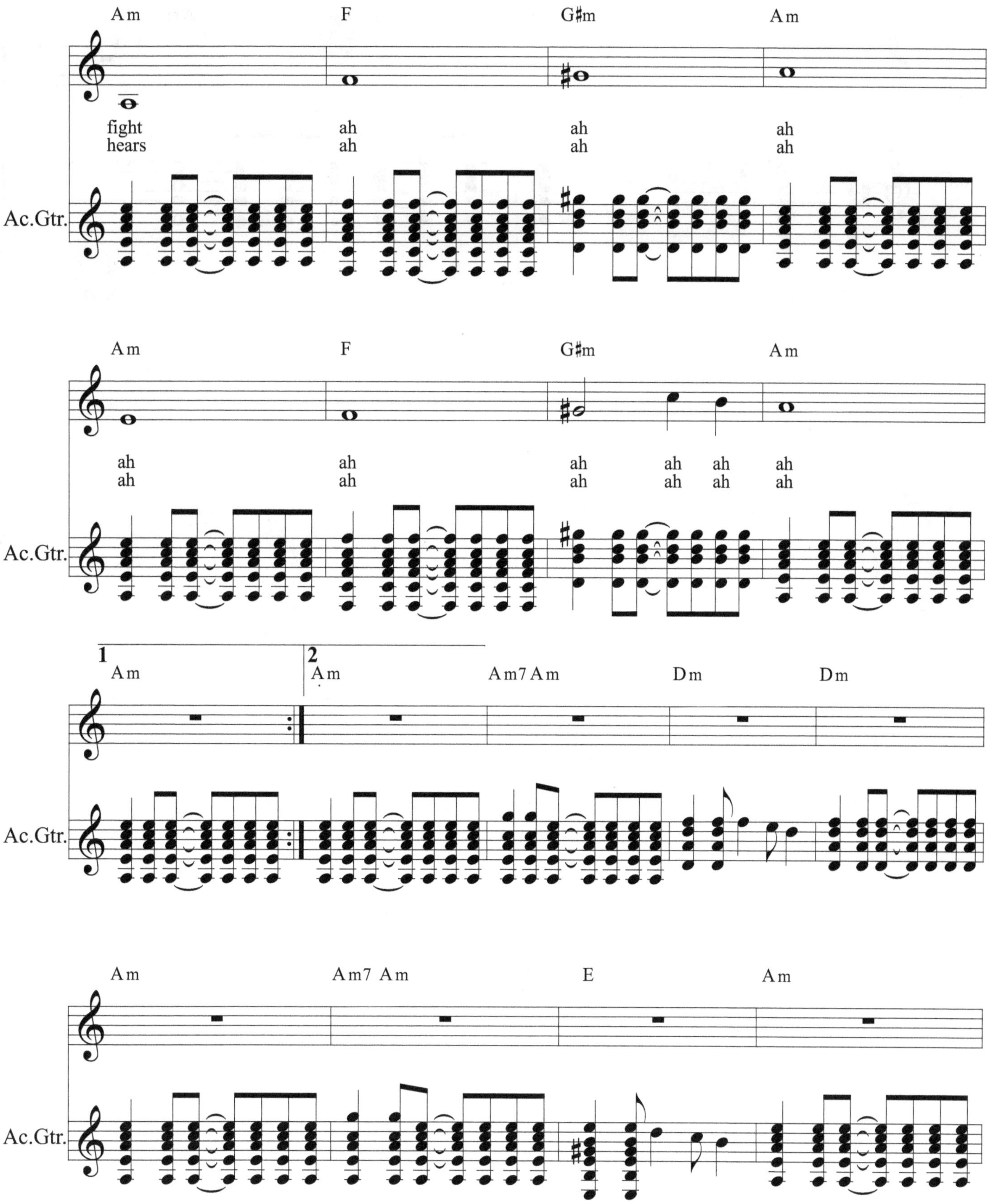
Am F G♯m Am
fight ah ah ah
hears ah ah ah
Ac.Gtr.
Am F G♯m Am
ah ah ah ah ah ah
ah ah ah ah ah ah
Ac.Gtr.
1 Am
2 Am Am7 Am Dm Dm
Ac.Gtr.
Am Am7 Am E Am
Ac.Gtr.

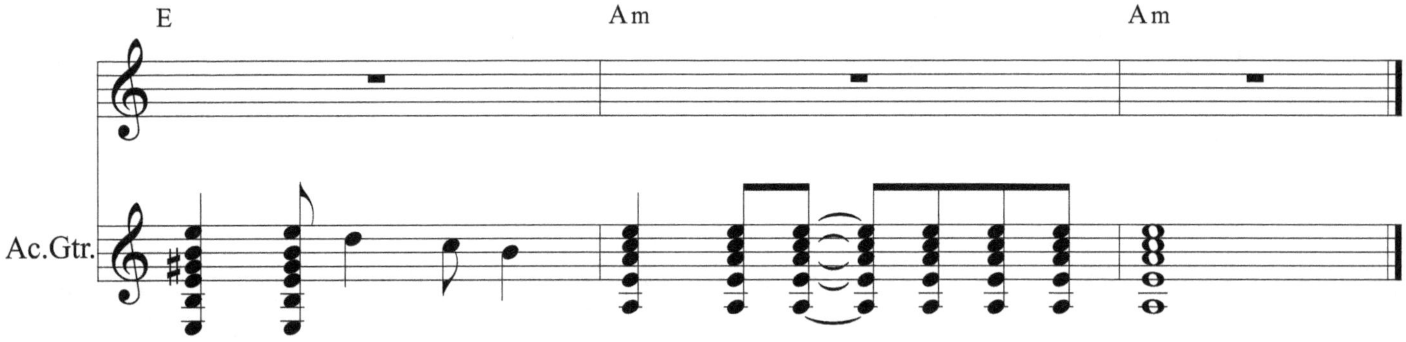
E
Am
Am
Ac.Gtr.

# I Love You, But

Helen Lapakko

Lyrics:
Oh I love you _____ but now _____ you are go — ne from me _____ I

saw you in the wak - ing of my

pa - in I called to you and

ri - ght a way you

ca me Oh. I love you but

now you are go - ne

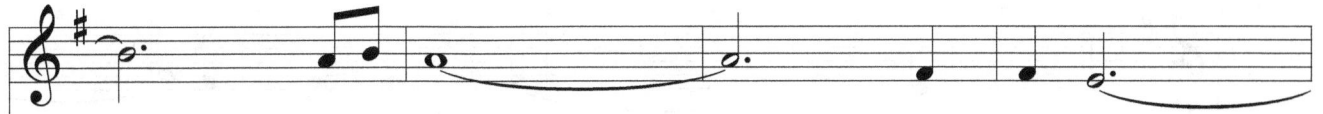

85

Esus4
Cmaj7
your ar - ms
Oh I love you
Ac.Gtr.
Asus/D
Em Em9
but now
you are go - ne
Ac.Gtr.
Em/G Em9
Em Em9
Em/G Em9
Cmaj7
Ac.Gtr.
Gmaj7
Asus/G
Ac.Gtr.
Esus4
Cmaj7
Ac.Gtr.

Asus/D
Em Em9 Em/G Em9 Em Em9
Ac.Gtr.
Em/G Em9 Cmaj7 Gmaj7
The others they beckon -
Ac.Gtr.
Asus/D Esus4
ed you a - way
Ac.Gtr.
Cmaj7 Asus/D
you said to me I'll see you on some
Ac.Gtr.
Em Em9 Em/G Em9 Cmaj7
o - ther rain - y day Then you loved me
Ac.Gtr.

but then _____ you ___ went _____

a - way _____ Oh I love you _____

but now _____ you are go - ne _____

Oh I

88

love you _____  but now _____ you are go - ne _____

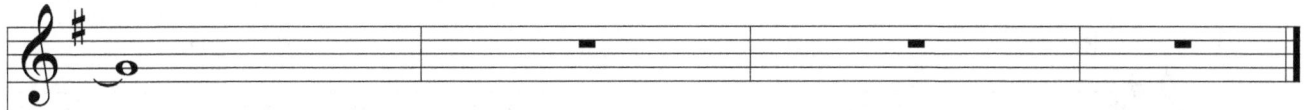

# I Met Him On a Touring Ship

Helen Lapakko

He touch - es my face and looks in - to my eyes He brush - es my hair back and gives me a smile He says so

quiet-ly the words I need to hear he com-forts my

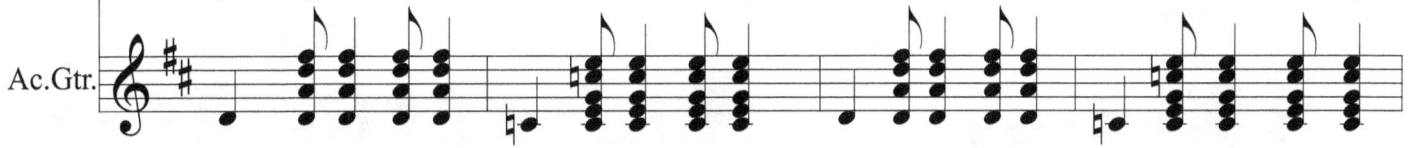

soul and_____ takes a-way the fear

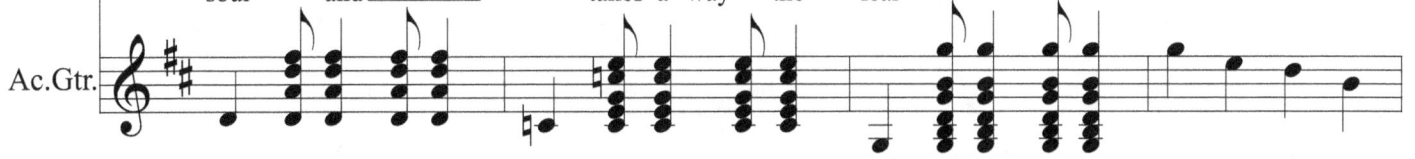

I met him on a tour-ing ship as I wan-dered and sang my songs_____

His spark-ling eyes and charm - ing smile made me feel like I be-longed_____

Then so gent-ly his lips brush my
I remember see-ing him that fir - st

91

cheek / night — I be-gin to melt / His hand-some face — my knees grow — / held hu - mor and

weak / light — He is like a whis-per / Now he lies next to you have to lis-ten / me — all — to / night

hear / long — he is al - ways in my heart — / this man who helps me — I keep him / find my —

near / song — I met him on a tour-ing ship

92

Lyrics under the staves:

as I wan-dered and sang my songs___ His spark-ling eyes and charm - ing smile

made me feel like I be-longed___ Some-times he

snores and some - times we fight But in the cold

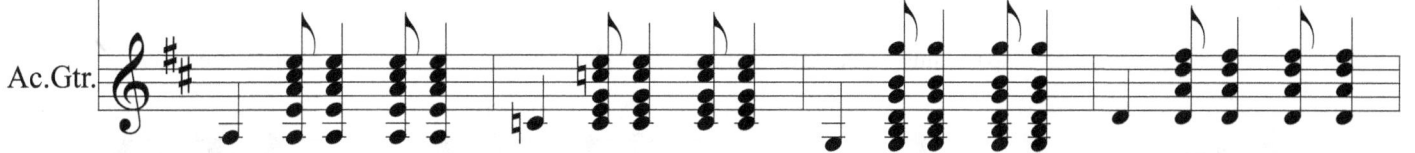

win - ter months his warmth is just right Now he sits

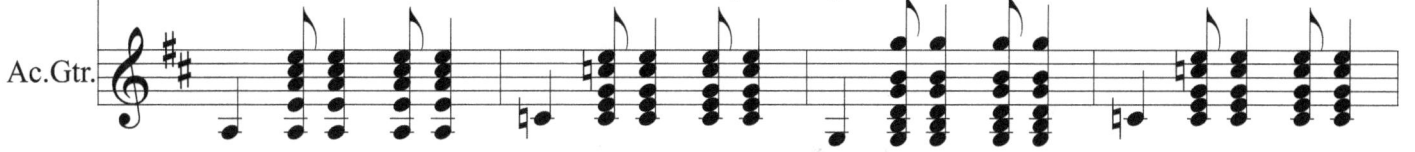

near me and I watch him re - ad This gent - le

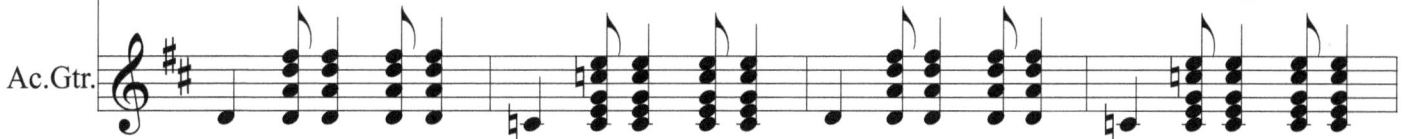

man of mine_____ is all I need

I met him on a tour-ing ship as I wan-dered and sang my songs_____

His spark-ling eyes and charm - ing smile made me feel like

I be - longed_____

# I Wonder

Helen Lapakko

Oh I

won-der ... if you're think-in' of me to-night

Oh Yes I won-der ... If you're think-in' of

95

me to-night to - night to - night   Oh the   kiss on my lips _____ lin-gers for ____
look for __ you _____ ev - ry   where

you my love _____   My   hun-gry eyes _____ bring your vi - sion
that I go _____   my   bo-dy yearns _____ just to

in my soul _____   My   kiss it trem - bles _____ un -
feel your touch _____   it   burns with pas - sion _____ to

til my bo - dy can't sleep a-ny-more  Oh I    won-der
feel you next to___ me    to - me   Oh I    won-der

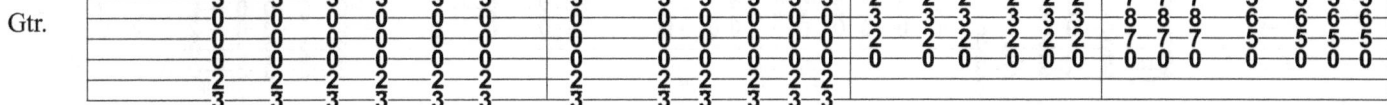

if you're think-in' of    me  to - night        Oh Yes I        won-der

If you're think-in' of    me to-night to - night  to - night  Oh I

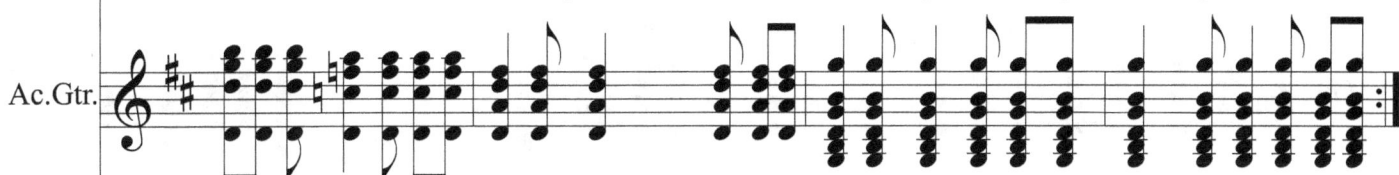

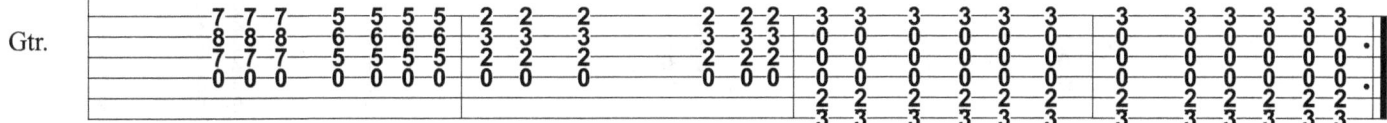

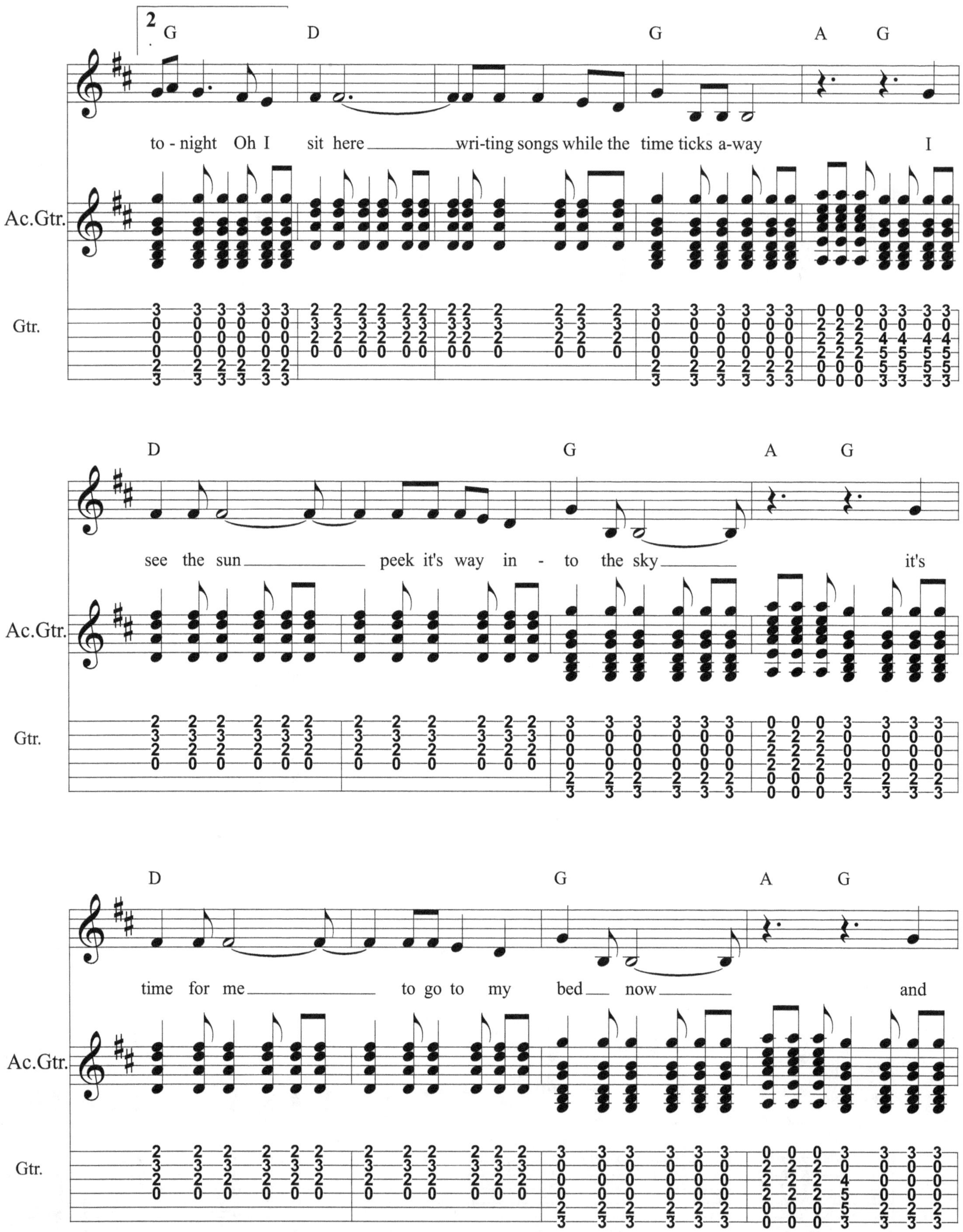

2
G D G A G
to - night Oh I sit here wri-ting songs while the time ticks a-way I
Ac.Gtr.
Gtr.
D G A G
see the sun peek it's way in - to the sky it's
Ac.Gtr.
Gtr.
D G A G
time for me to go to my bed now and
Ac.Gtr.
Gtr.

dream of you_____        and the kiss I want so__much    so much   Oh   I

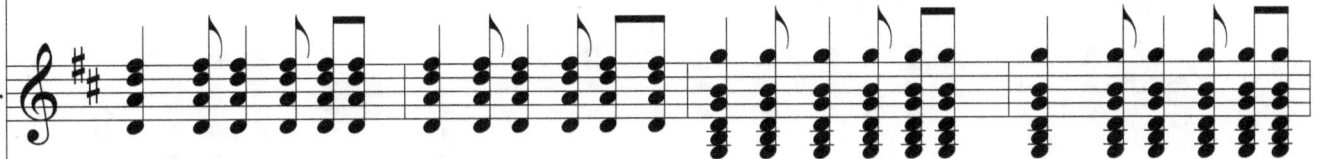

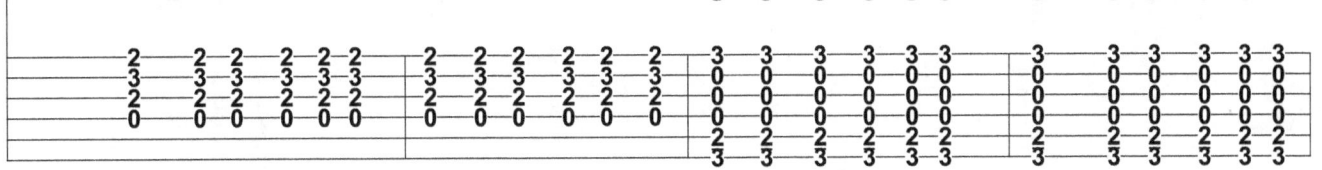

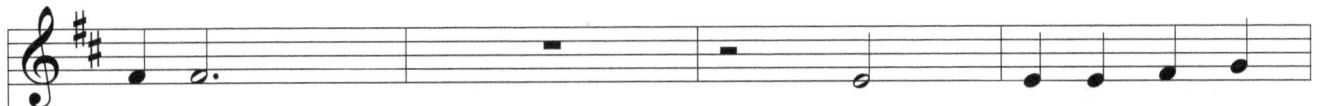

won - der                                    Last        night   it   felt   so

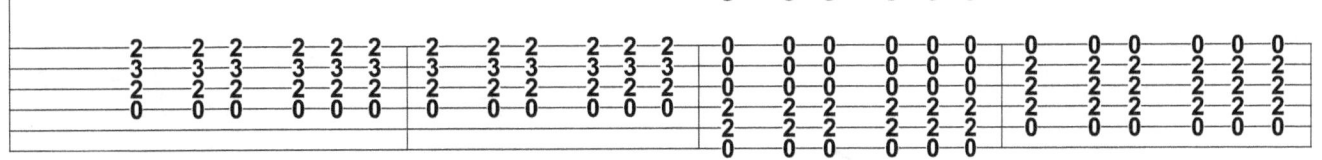

re - al_____        The   touch  of  your    hand  gave  me   a

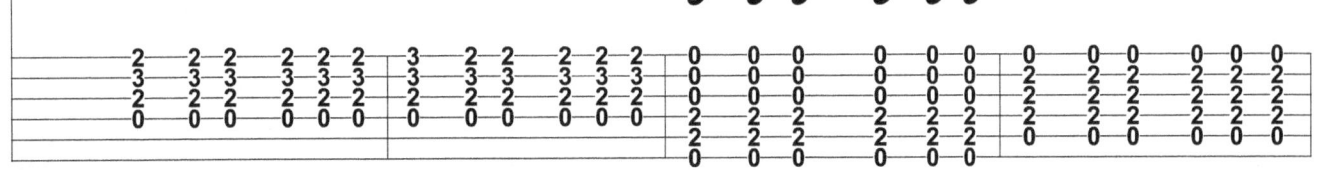

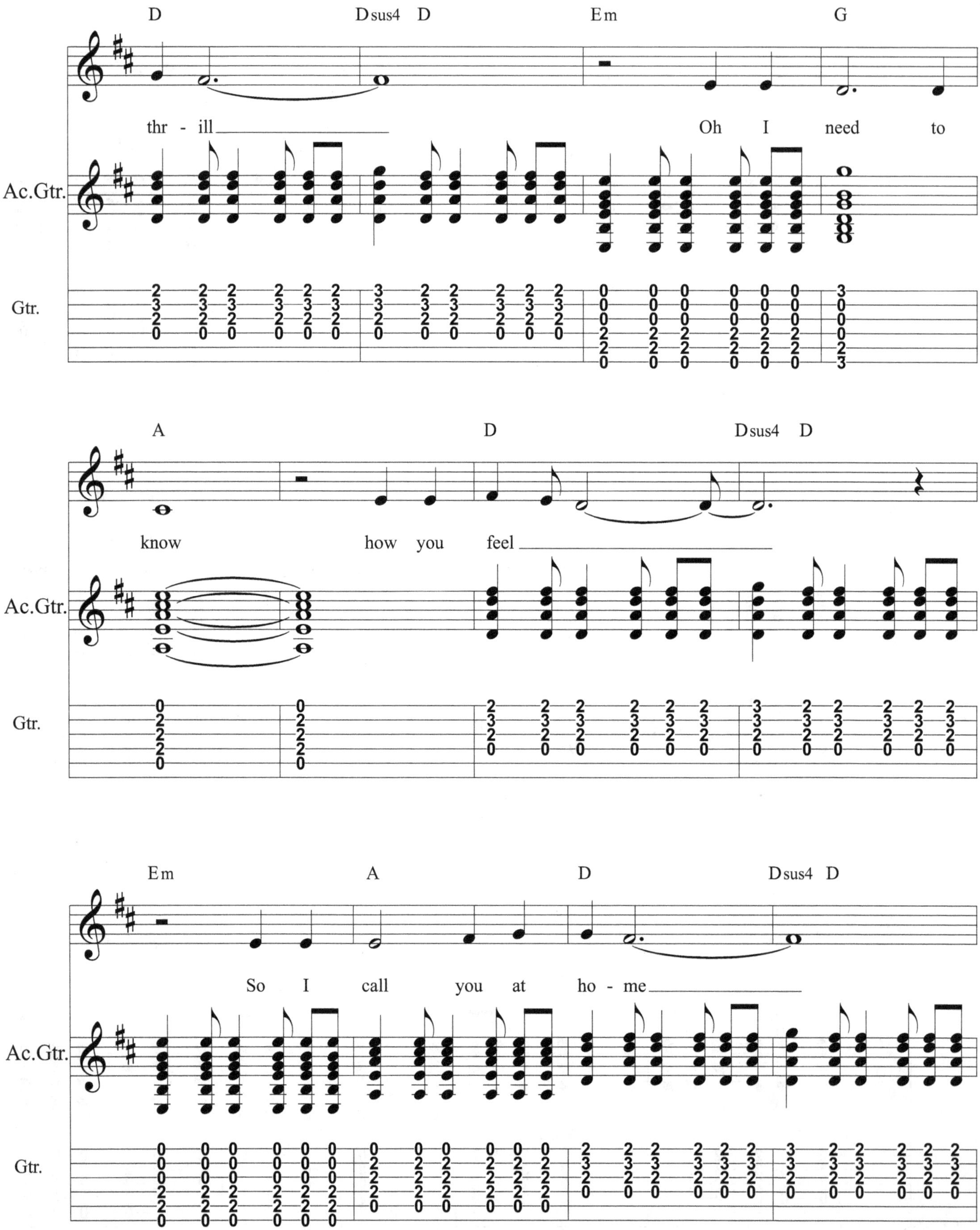
D Dsus4 D Em G
thr - ill Oh I need to
Ac.Gtr.
Gtr.
A D Dsus4 D
know how you feel
Ac.Gtr.
Gtr.
Em A D Dsus4 D
So I call you at ho - me
Ac.Gtr.
Gtr.

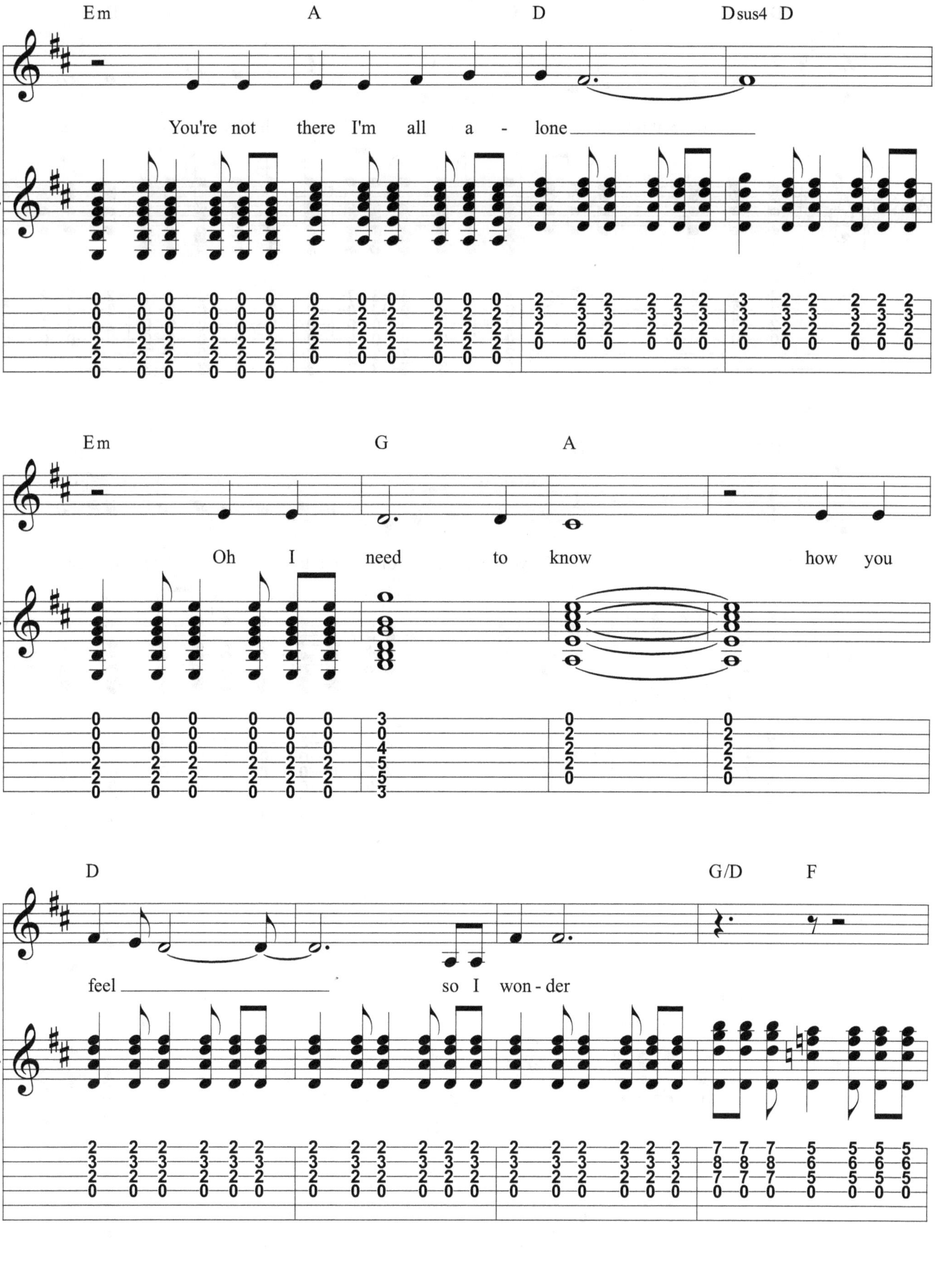
Em A D Dsus4 D
You're not there I'm all a - lone
Ac.Gtr.
Gtr.
Em G A
Oh I need to know how you
Ac.Gtr.
Gtr.
D G/D F
feel so I won - der
Ac.Gtr.
Gtr.

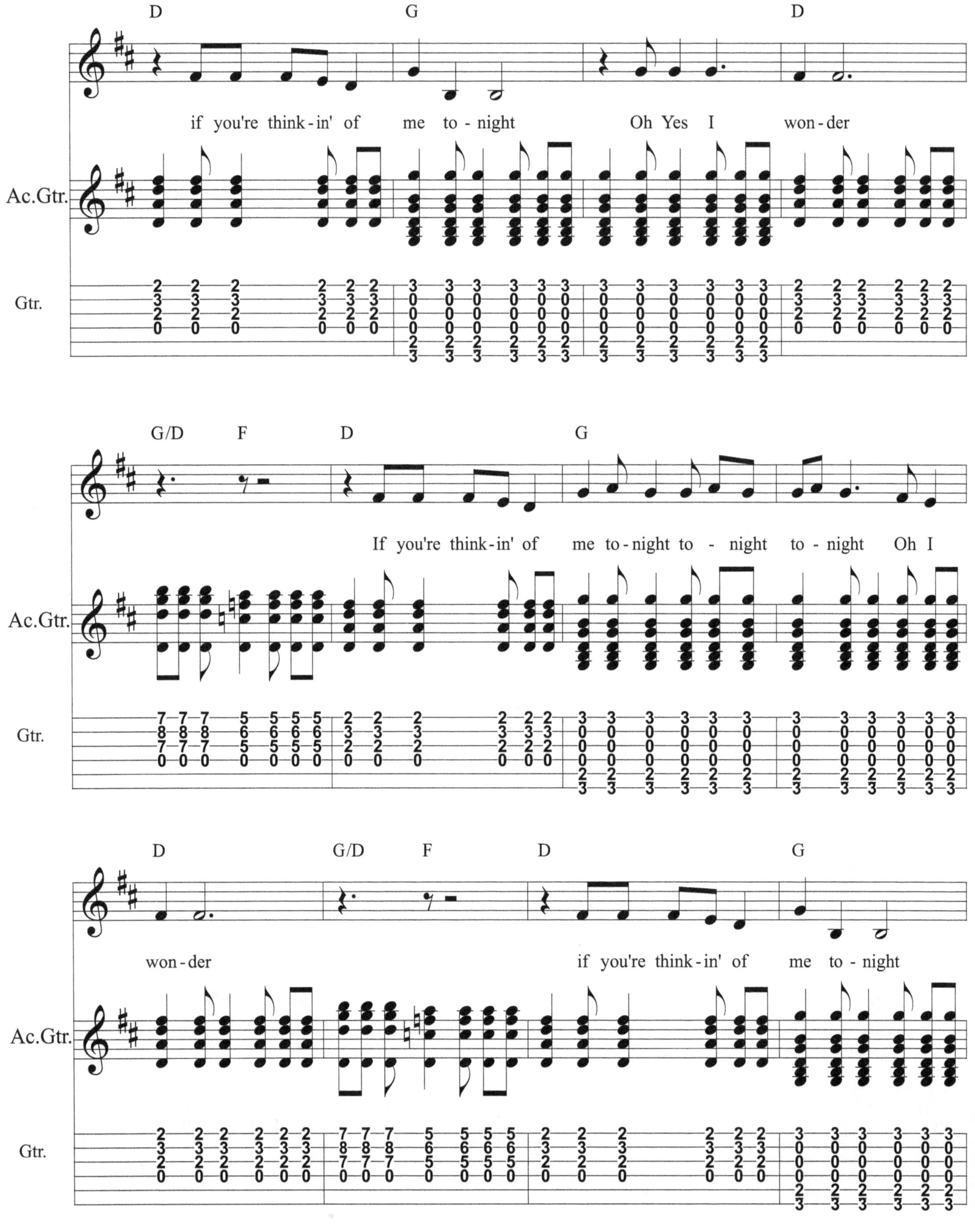
D G D
if you're think-in' of me to-night Oh Yes I won-der
Ac.Gtr.
Gtr.
G/D F D G
If you're think-in' of me to-night to - night to - night Oh I
Ac.Gtr.
Gtr.
D G/D F D G
won-der if you're think-in' of me to - night
Ac.Gtr.
Gtr.

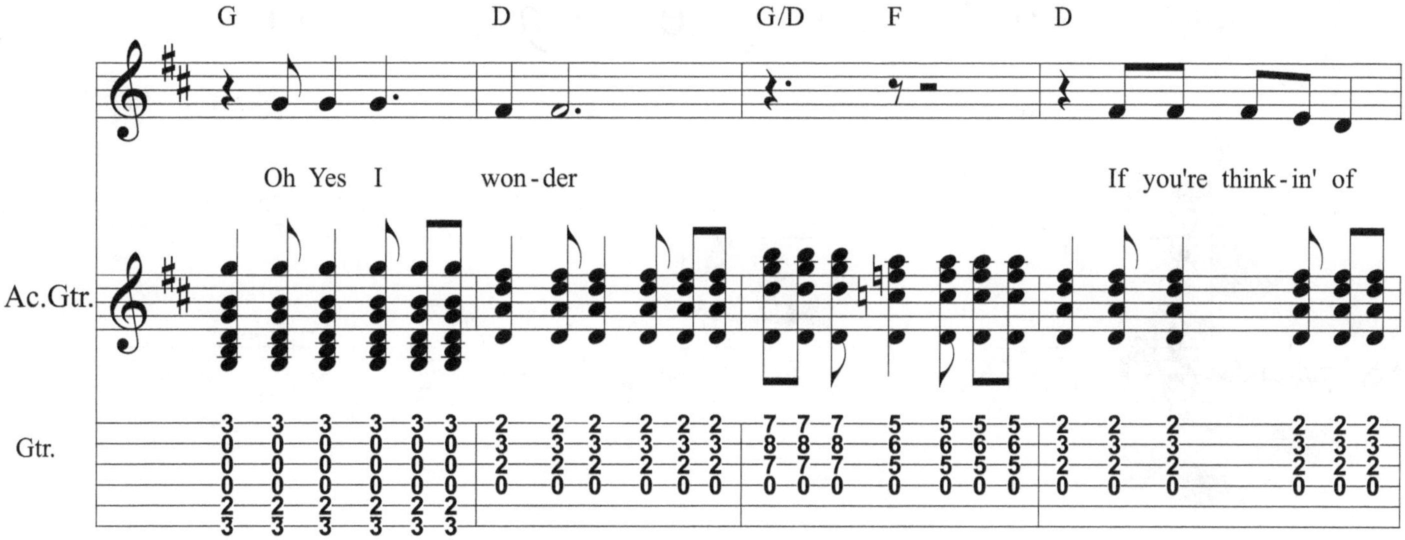
G D G/D F D
Oh Yes I won-der If you're think-in' of
Ac.Gtr.
Gtr.

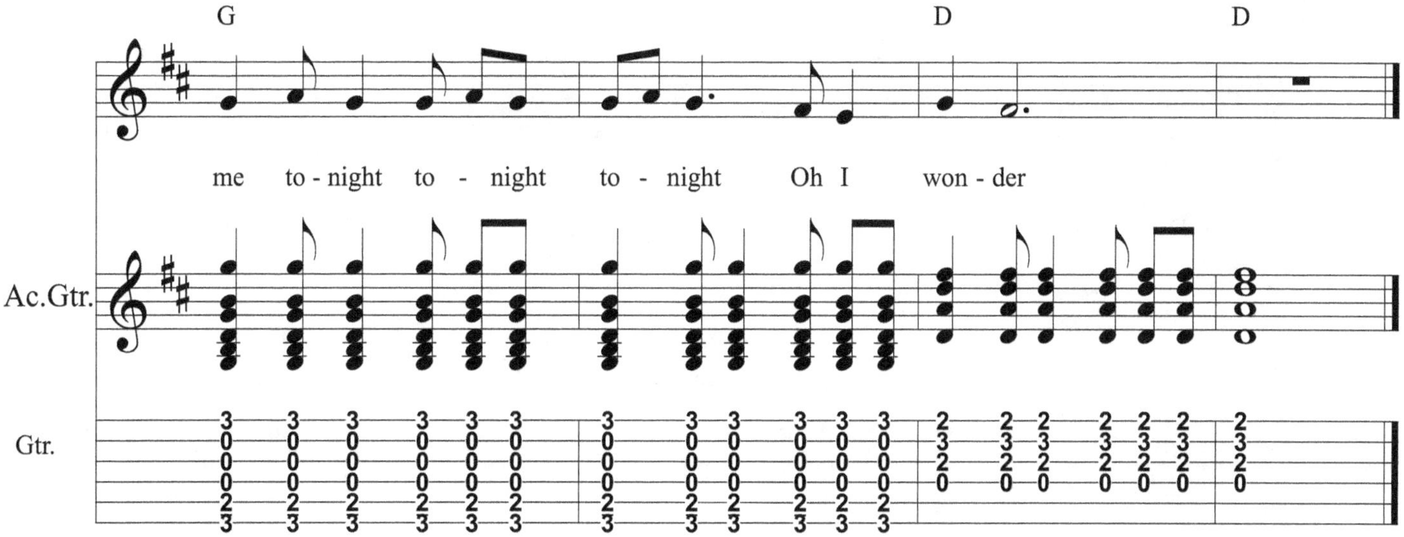
G D D
me to-night to - night to - night Oh I won-der
Ac.Gtr.
Gtr.

# I'm Gonna Write Me a Sexy Song

Helen Lapakko

I'm gon-na write me a

sex-y song_____ One I can sing all night long_____ bout the cow-boy I

met last night_____ looked so good with his jeans so tight_____

1. I watched him dan-cin in that coun - try____ line
2. His cow - boy hat____ looked so good on him
3. When the night end-ed he said your place or mine

I think I'm gon - na make him__ mi - ne
I think I heard someone call him__ Jim__
got me a twelve pack and plen-ty of time

105

G　　　　　　C　　　　　　Am　　　　D

Then＿ he＿ grabbed me for a　coun - try＿ swing
I wanted to＿ touch＿ his　dirty three day beard
we spent the night talk - in'＿ we　watched the sun rise

Ac.Gtr.

*H*

G　　　　　　C　　　　　　Am　　　　D

My feet were＿ fly - in' I just　wan - ted to sing＿
I's glad when he turned and said　would ya like a beer＿
I sure loved＿ look-in in those　big＿ blue - eyes＿

Ac.Gtr.

*H*

D　　A　　G　　　　D　　A

＿　I'm gon-na write me a sex-y song＿　One I can sing

Ac.Gtr.

G　　　　D　　A　　G　　　　D　　A

all night long＿　bout the cow-boy I met last night＿　looked so good with his

Ac.Gtr.

106

G 1,2 G 3 G G C
jeans so tight now we go dan-cin'
Ac.Gtr.
H
Am D G C
ev-er-y night He knows how to swing me
Ac.Gtr.
H
Am D G C
round the floor just right My bel-ly is grow-iin'
Ac.Gtr.
H
Am D G C
now that's a good sign Yes, we got mar-ried
Ac.Gtr.
H

I made him mine ____ Now I'm singin' my

sex-y song ____ One I can sing all night long ____ bout the cow-boy I

met that night ____ looked so good with his jeans so tight ____

Now I'm sing-in' my sex-y song ____

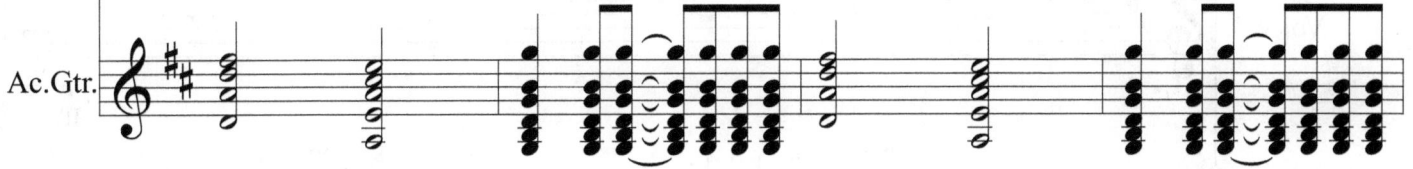

yes i'm sing-in' my sex-y song _____ now I'm sing-in' my sex-y song to-

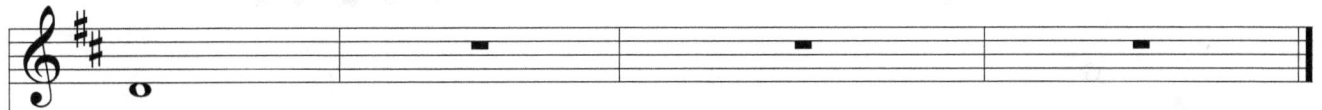

night

109

# It's a Saturday Night

Helen Lapakko

*Use bar chords

Lyrics:

sat-ur-day night and it's a quar-ter past two_____ walk-in' down the street I ain't got no shoes_____ Don't know where I'm go-in' don't know where I've been look-in' a-round I can't find me a friend

Lyrics under the staves:

Went to the bar with my good friend Jill _____ Then she left with some
Put my purse _____ down _____ on the floor _____ danced with some guy he was

guy named Bill _____ Left _____ me sit-tin' there all a-lone wond-rin' how I'm
six foot four _____ When I got back my wallet was gone I closed my eyes

1
gon-na get home _____

2
this was just wrong It's a _____ Sat-ur-day night _____ it's a

quar-ter past two _____ my mon-ey's gone _____ my

111

good friend too

Then some sex - y dark haired man looked at me and he
Lights went up I saw his hand he was wearing a

grabbed my hand I kicked off my shoes and danced all night
wed - ding band I grabbed my purse walked the door

**1**
I had found mis - ter right
left my shoes on the

**2**
dance room floor it's a Sat - ur - day night

it's a quar-ter past two ... mis-ter right is gone

I ain't got no shoes

Got my cell phone it was dead____
Some guy pulled up said wan-na ride____

star-ted walk-in' to clear my head____ too ma-ny drinks not e-nough food
took one look wanted to run and hide I stood up tall said not__ to - night

113

Lyrics:

**1.** could-n't fig - ure out what I need-ed to do
**2.** walked a - way fast to a - void a fight It's a _____

Sat - ur - day night

it's a quar - ter past two

My cell phone's dead

I'm feel - in' blue

Turned the cor - ner saw cra - zy Joe _____

G C9 Eb9 D9 C9
com-in' down the street He was walk-in' real slow talk-in' to him-self wav-in' a
Ac.Gtr.
Eb9 D9 C9 Eb9 D9 C9 Eb9 D9 C9 G
gun in the air walked right by like I was-n't there
Ac.Gtr.
C9 G C9
It's a Sat-ur-day night and it's a quar-ter past two
Ac.Gtr.
G C9 Eb9 D9 C9
walk-in down the street I ain't got no shoes I don't know where I'm go-in'
Ac.Gtr.

Eb9　D9　C9　Eb9　D9　C9　Eb9　D9　C9

don't know where I've been　look-in' a - round can't　find　me a friend It's a

G　C9　G　C9

Sat - ur - day night　it's a quar-ter past two　Don't

G　C9　G　C9

have a ride　I ain't got no shoes　It's a

G　C9　G　C9

Sat - ur - day night　my cell phone's dead　My

116

Lyrics under the staves:

mon-ney's gone    can't feel my head    It's a

Sat - ur day night    It's a Sat-ur day ni - ght    It's a

Sat - ur-day night    It's a Sat-ur-day ni - gh - t

# Last Night I Had a Dream

Helen Lapakko

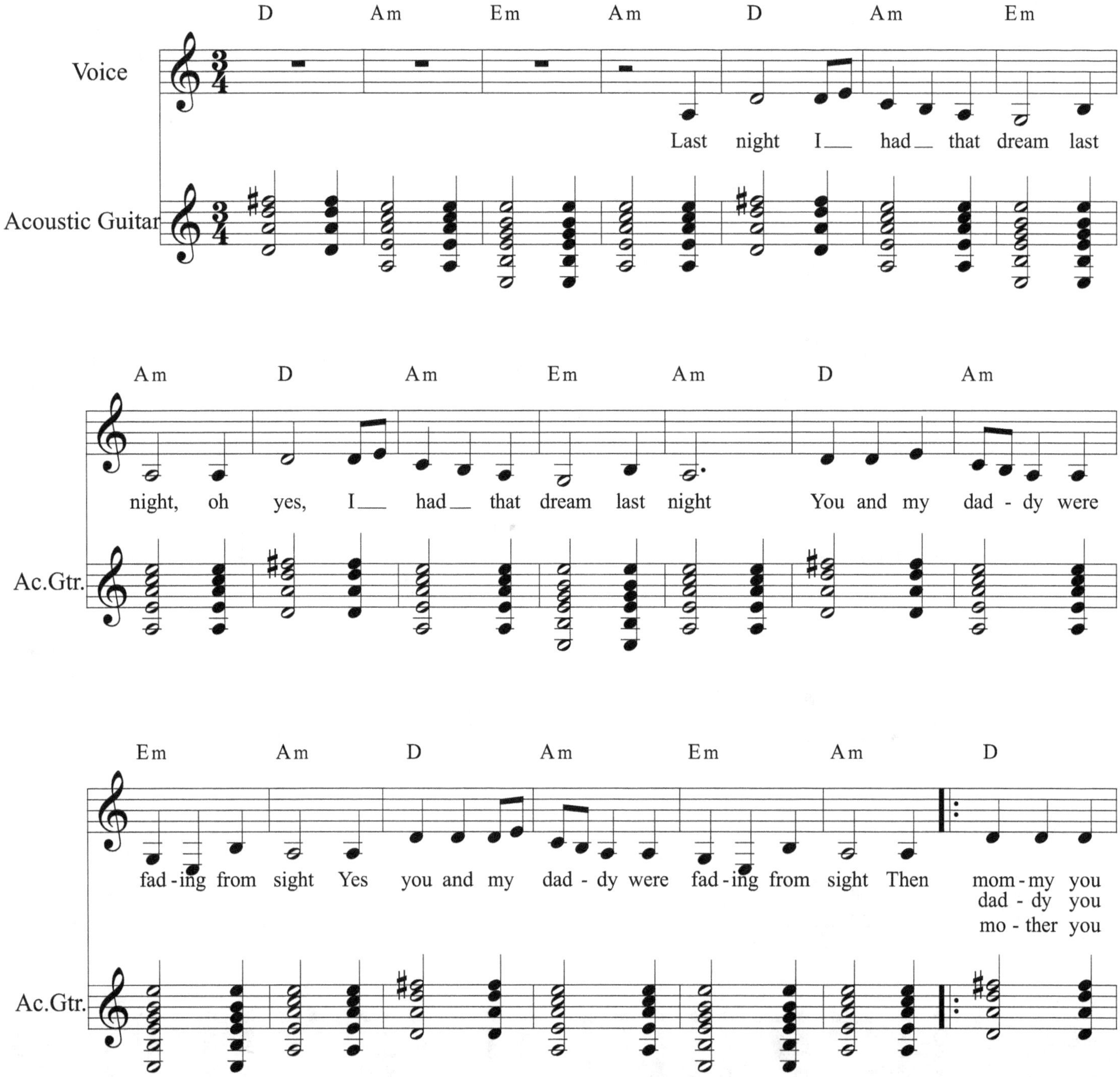
D Am Em Am D Am Em
Voice
Last night I had that dream last
Acoustic Guitar
Am D Am Em Am D Am
night, oh yes, I had that dream last night You and my dad - dy were
Ac.Gtr.
Em Am D Am Em Am D
fad - ing from sight Yes you and my dad - dy were fad - ing from sight Then mom - my you
dad - dy you
mo - ther you
Ac.Gtr.

**Line 1** (Chords: C D C D C D)

said oh — daugh - ter dear, I wish you were with me I want you so
just kept walk - ing a - way you ne - ver looked back you had no - thing to
said yes — daugh - ter it's true I know what — happen - ed what he did to

**Line 2** (Chords: C D C D C D)

near, I'm sor - ry for all of those things we did wrong, your pre - cious —
say you're shroud - ed in pain you — don't no - tice me not a flick - er of —
you I wish I could change it and make it all right he — robbed you of your

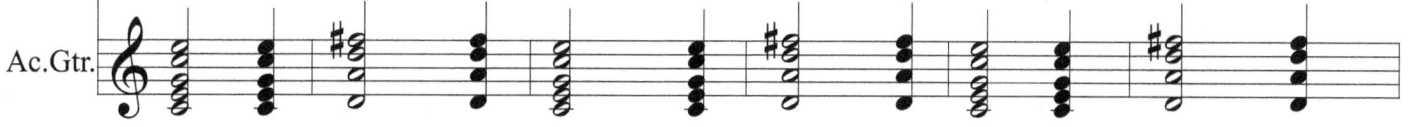

**Line 3** (Chords: C D C D C D C)

child - hood now — is gone. Oh daugh - ter I must leave I must go a - way the
love from you can I see Oh dad - dy who are you, oh what is in - side I'm
in - no - cence so late at night Oh daugh - ter I must leave I must go a - way the

**Line 4** (Chords: D C D C D)

pain is too great now I just can't stay I'm sor - ry so sor - ry last
so sca - red of you I run and I hide oh dad - dy dear dad - dy last
pain is too great now I just can't stay I'm sor - ry so sor - ry last

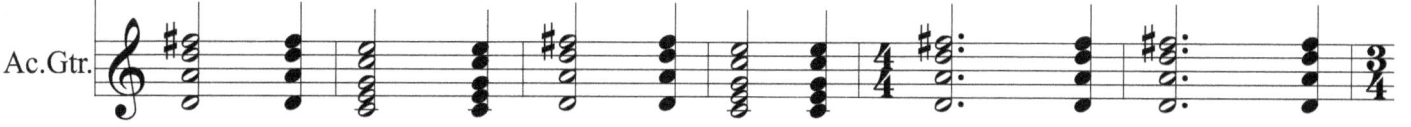

119

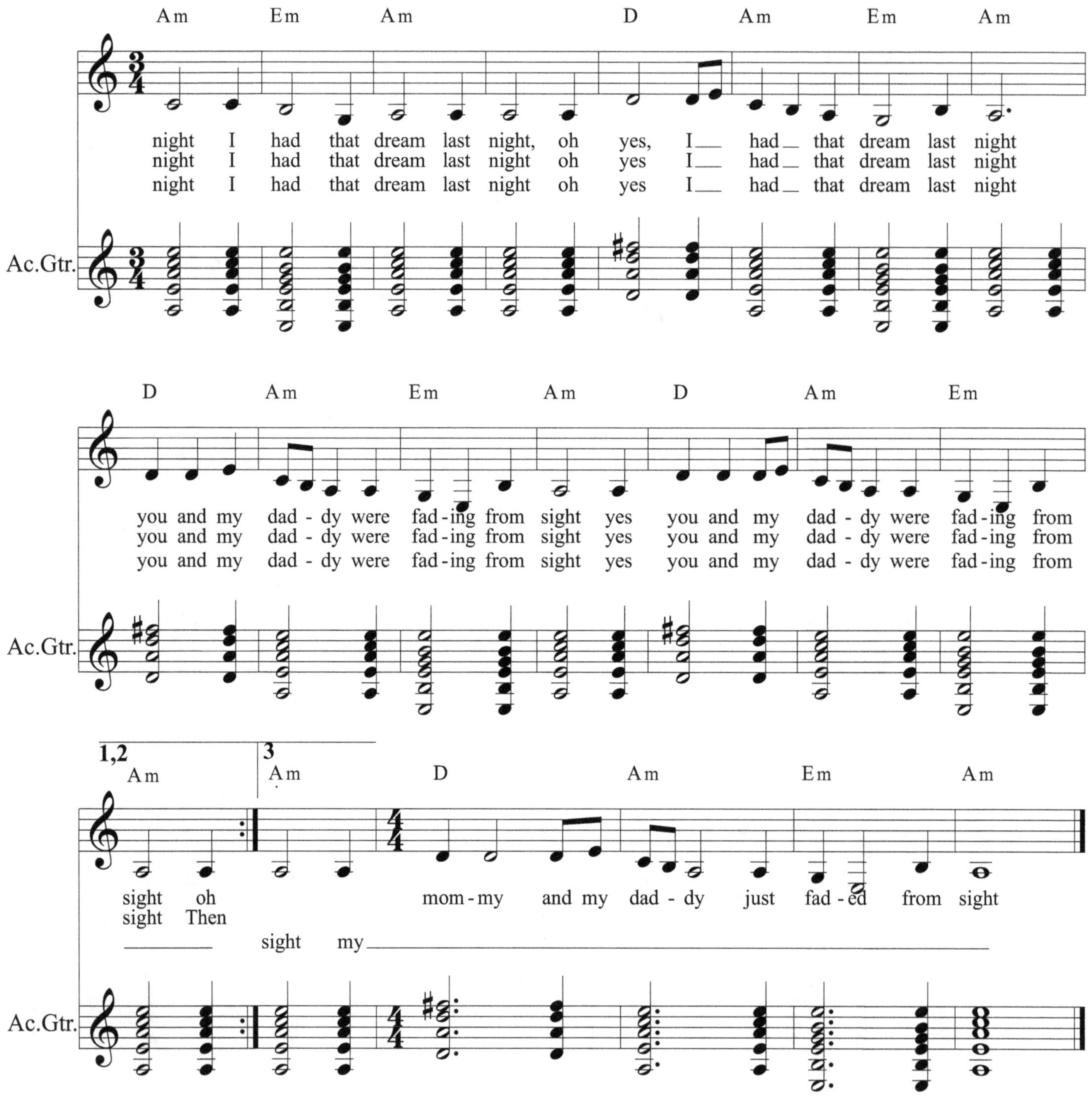

# Life and Love Go On

Helen Lapakko

Lyrics:
We were to - geth - er a - lone last night

You loved me long you held me so tight last

night so warm and gen tle

and lo ving were you    Now the night is o ver

does it mean we're through    me and you

well, life and love go on

yeah life and love go on

You said you want-ed    to start a new life

Lyrics:

You said you were going to leave your wife and start a new

life

well does that mean

that your com-ing with me

or does that mean

that you want to be free with-out me

well, life and love go on

123

yeah life and love go on

Thank you sir for show-ing to me

what love can be like when you're real-ly free like

me Thank you for show-ing me

that love can be kind and that it is there

for me to find some - time

well, life and love go on

yeah life and love go on

so man-y have taught me what love is a - bout

At times it made me cry and oth-ers made me shout all a -

125

A · · · · · · · · · · · · · · · · · · · · · · · · · F · · · · · · · · · · · · · · C

bout · · · · · · · · · · · · · · · · · · · · · · · · for what love does · · give me

Ac.Gtr.

F · · · · · · · · · · · · · · C · · · · · · · · · · · · F · · · · · · · · · · · · · C

it makes me feel so a - live · · · · · · · · · I nev - er cease to · · want it

Ac.Gtr.

F · · · · · · · · · · · · · · C · · · · · · · · · · · · A

I · · need it to sur - vive and · · stay a · · · · live.

Ac.Gtr.

G · · · · · · · · · · · · · · D · · · · · · · · · · · · Em

well, life and · · love · · · · go · · · · on

Ac.Gtr.

G · · · · · · · · · · · · · · D · · · · · · · · Em A Em A · · Em A Em A · · Em

yeah life and · · love · · · · go · · · · on and on and · · on and on and · · on

Ac.Gtr.

# MY DADDY LEFT ME

Helen Lapakko

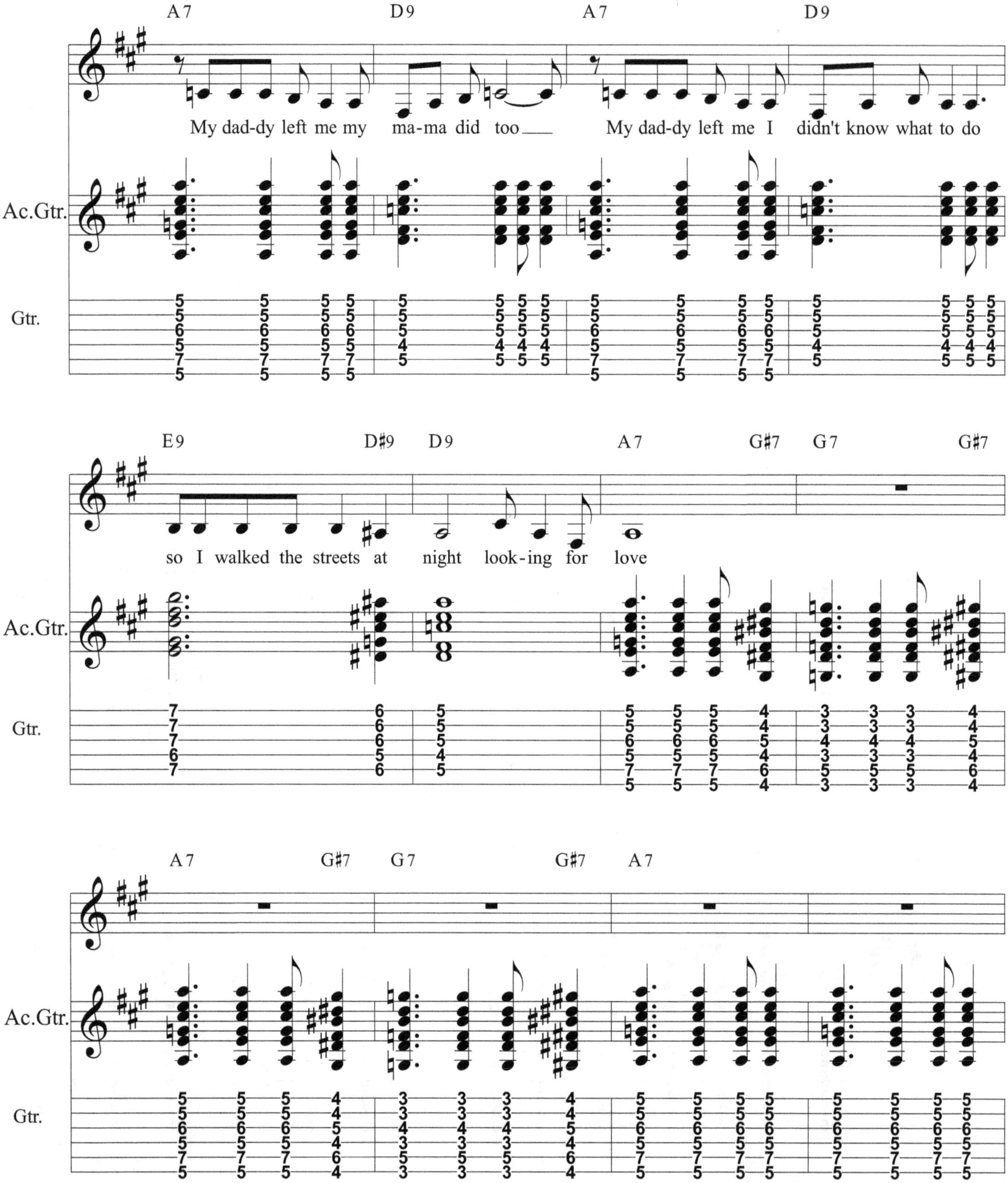
A7 D9 A7 D9
My dad-dy left me my ma-ma did too
My dad-dy left me I didn't know what to do
Ac.Gtr.
Gtr.
E9 D#9 D9 A7 G#7 G7 G#7
so I walked the streets at night look-ing for love
Ac.Gtr.
Gtr.
A7 G#7 G7 G#7 A7
Ac.Gtr.
Gtr.

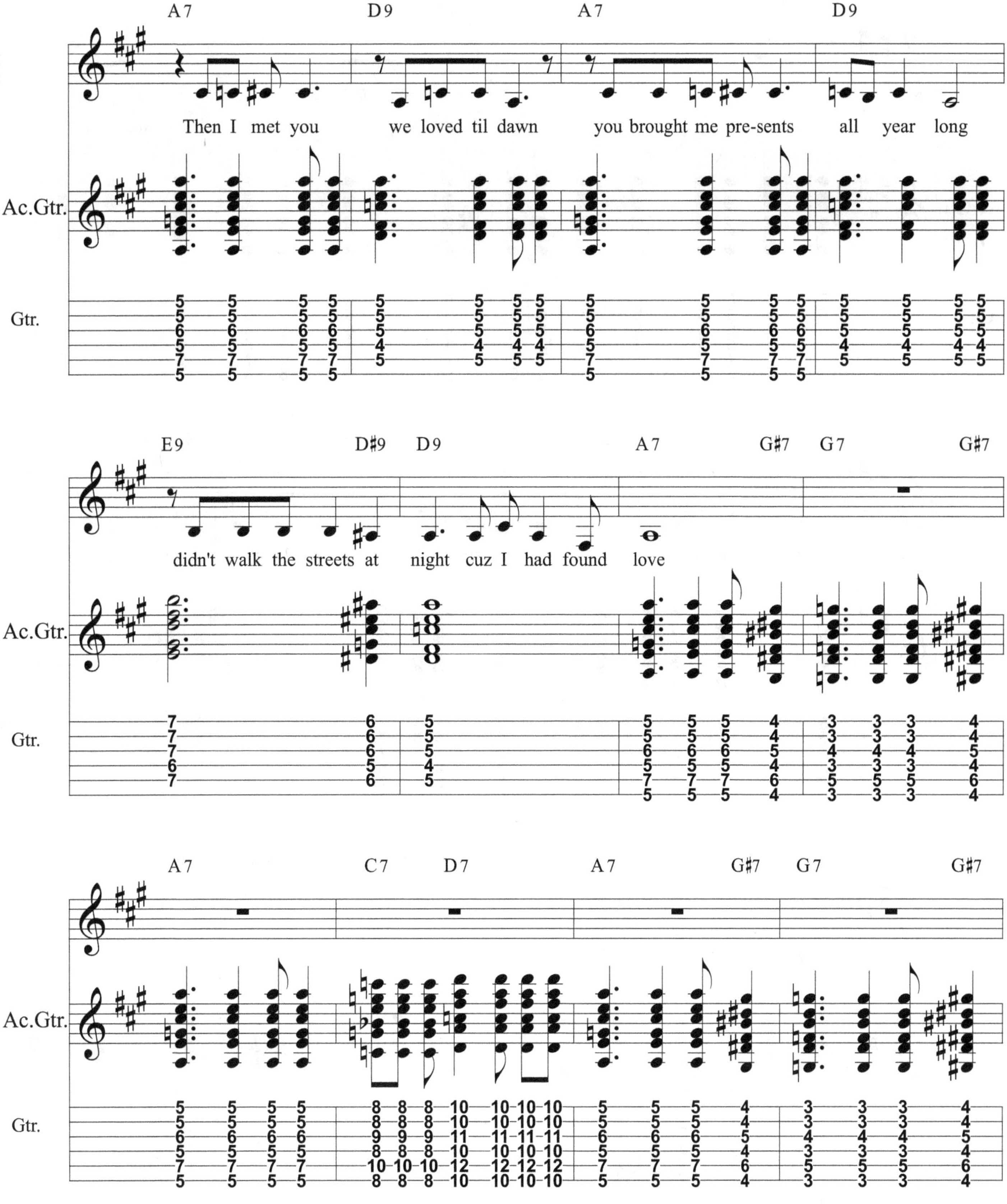
A7 D9 A7 D9
Then I met you we loved til dawn you brought me pre-sents all year long
Ac.Gtr.
Gtr.
E9 D♯9 D9 A7 G♯7 G7 G♯7
didn't walk the streets at night cuz I had found love
Ac.Gtr.
Gtr.
A7 C7 D7 A7 G♯7 G7 G♯7
Ac.Gtr.
Gtr.

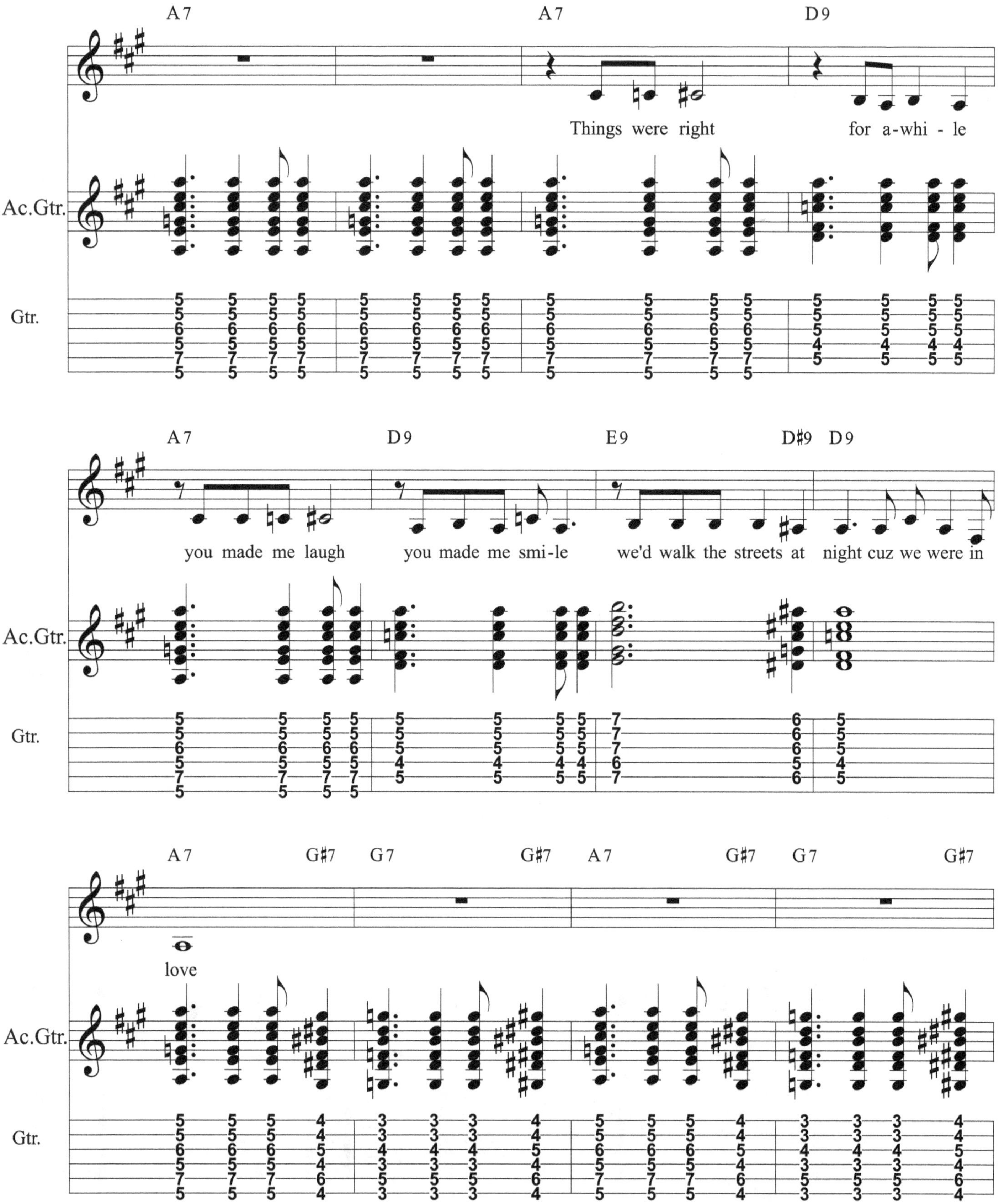
A7 A7 D9
Things were right for a-whi - le
Ac.Gtr.
Gtr.
A7 D9 E9 D#9 D9
you made me laugh you made me smi-le we'd walk the streets at night cuz we were in
Ac.Gtr.
Gtr.
A7 G#7 G7 G#7 A7 G#7 G7 G#7
love
Ac.Gtr.
Gtr.

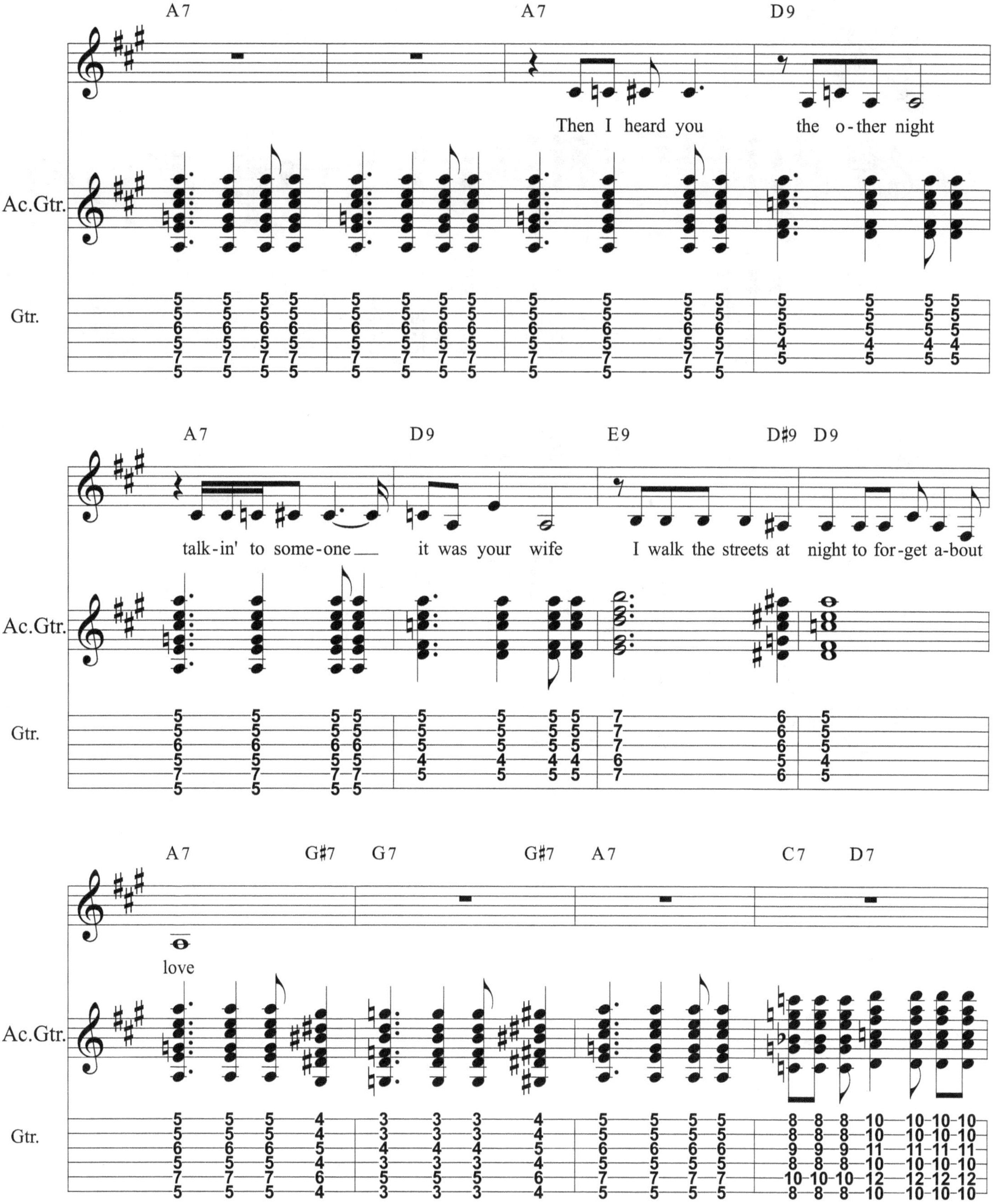
A7
A7
D9
Then I heard you the o-ther night
Ac.Gtr.
Gtr.
A7
D9
E9
D♯9 D9
talk-in' to some-one it was your wife I walk the streets at night to for-get a-bout
Ac.Gtr.
Gtr.
A7
G♯7
G7
G♯7
A7
C7
D7
love
Ac.Gtr.
Gtr.

The o-ther night talk-in' to some-one it was your wife

Then I heard you

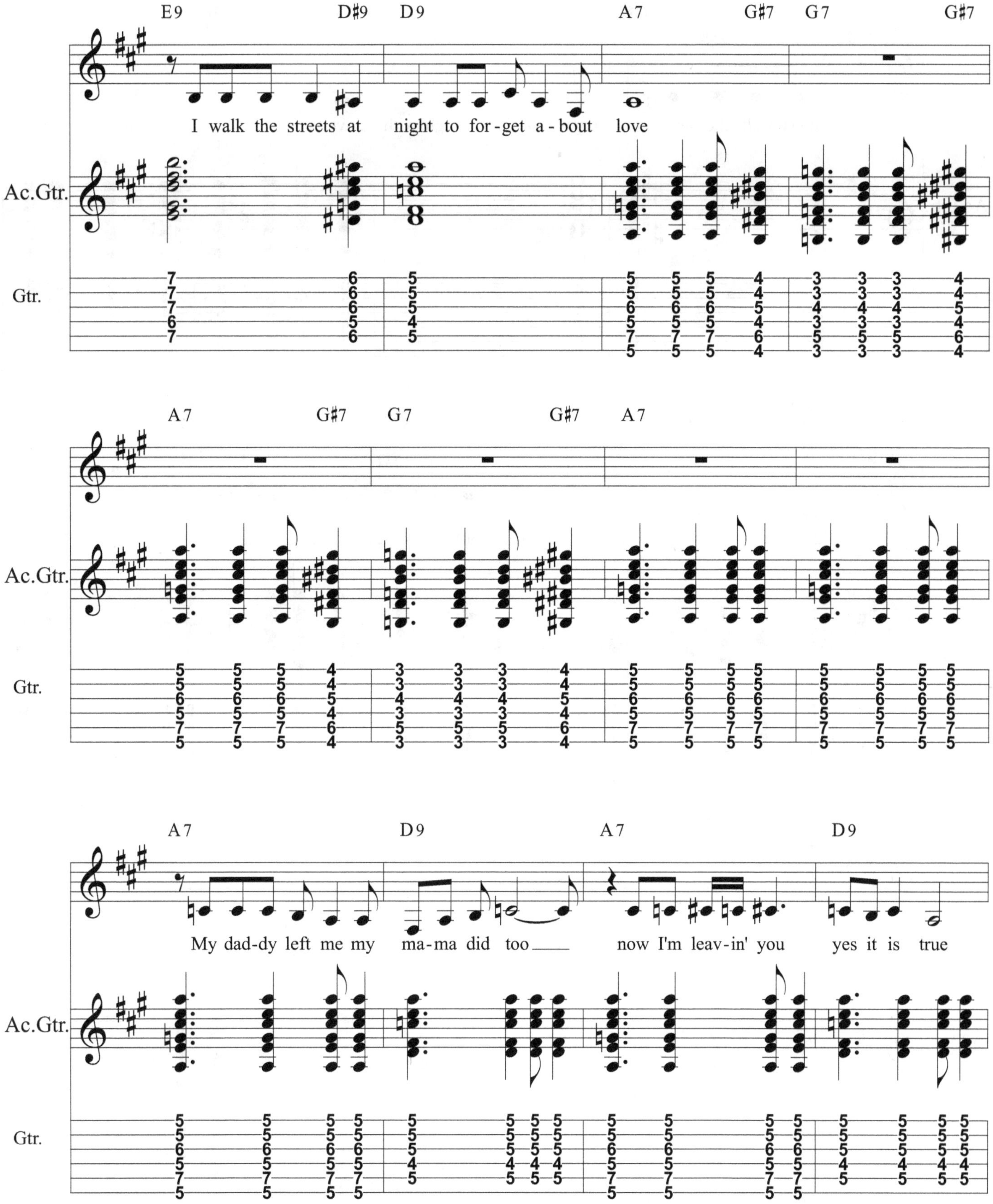
E9 D♯9 D9 A7 G♯7 G7 G♯7
I walk the streets at night to for-get a-bout love
Ac.Gtr.
Gtr.
A7 G♯7 G7 G♯7 A7
Ac.Gtr.
Gtr.
A7 D9 A7 D9
My dad-dy left me my ma-ma did too now I'm leav-in' you yes it is true
Ac.Gtr.
Gtr.

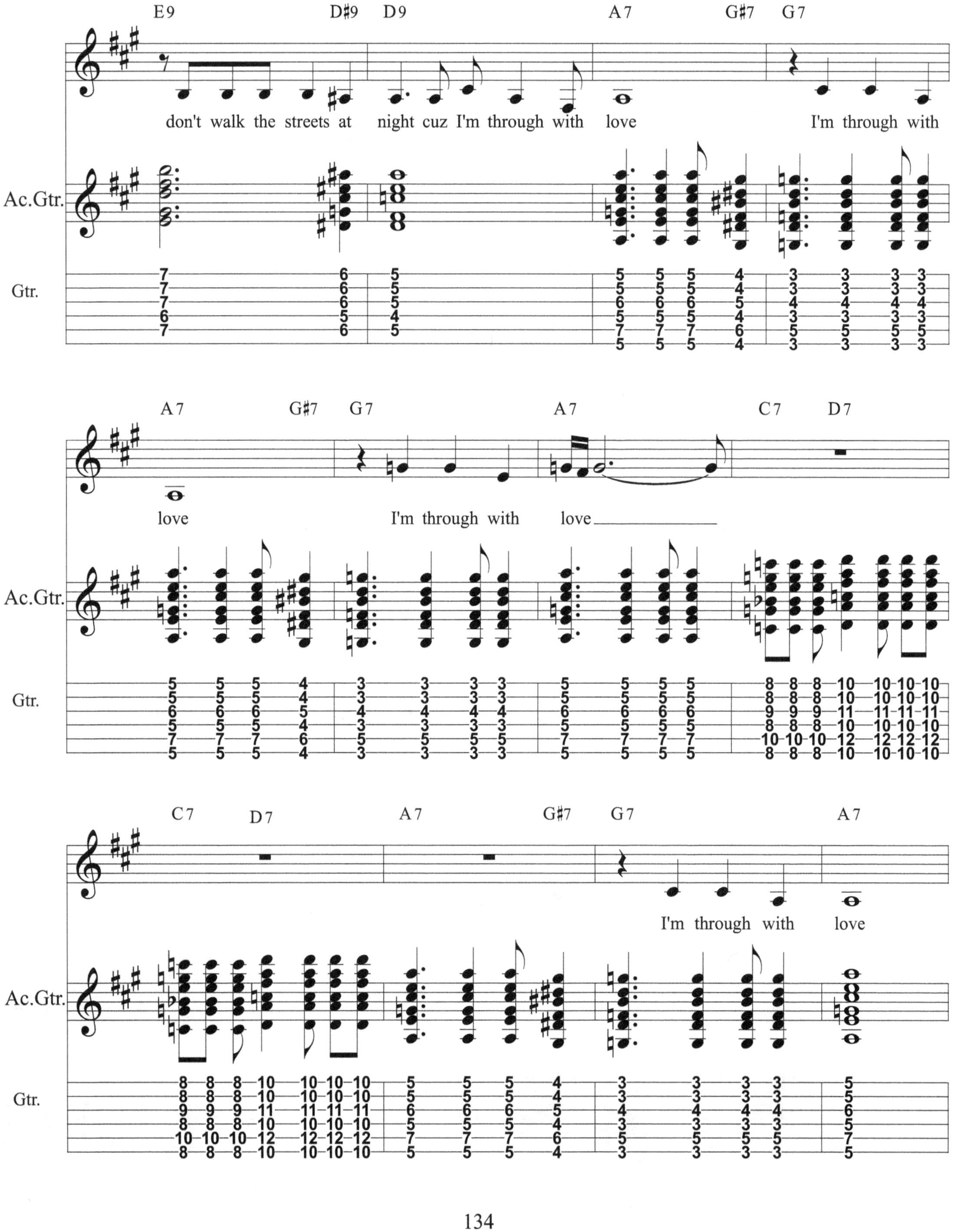
E9 D♯9 D9 A7 G♯7 G7
don't walk the streets at night cuz I'm through with love I'm through with
Ac.Gtr.
Gtr.
A7 G♯7 G7 A7 C7 D7
love I'm through with love
Ac.Gtr.
Gtr.
C7 D7 A7 G♯7 G7 A7
I'm through with love
Ac.Gtr.
Gtr.

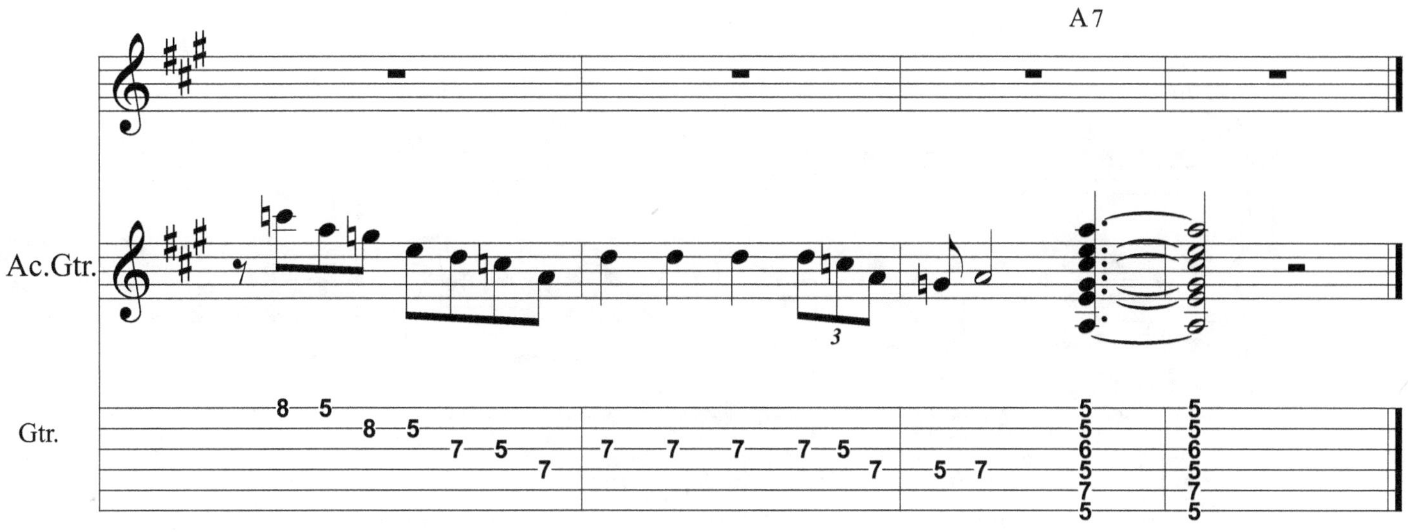
A 7
Ac.Gtr.
Gtr.

# Nature's Prayer

Helen Lapakko

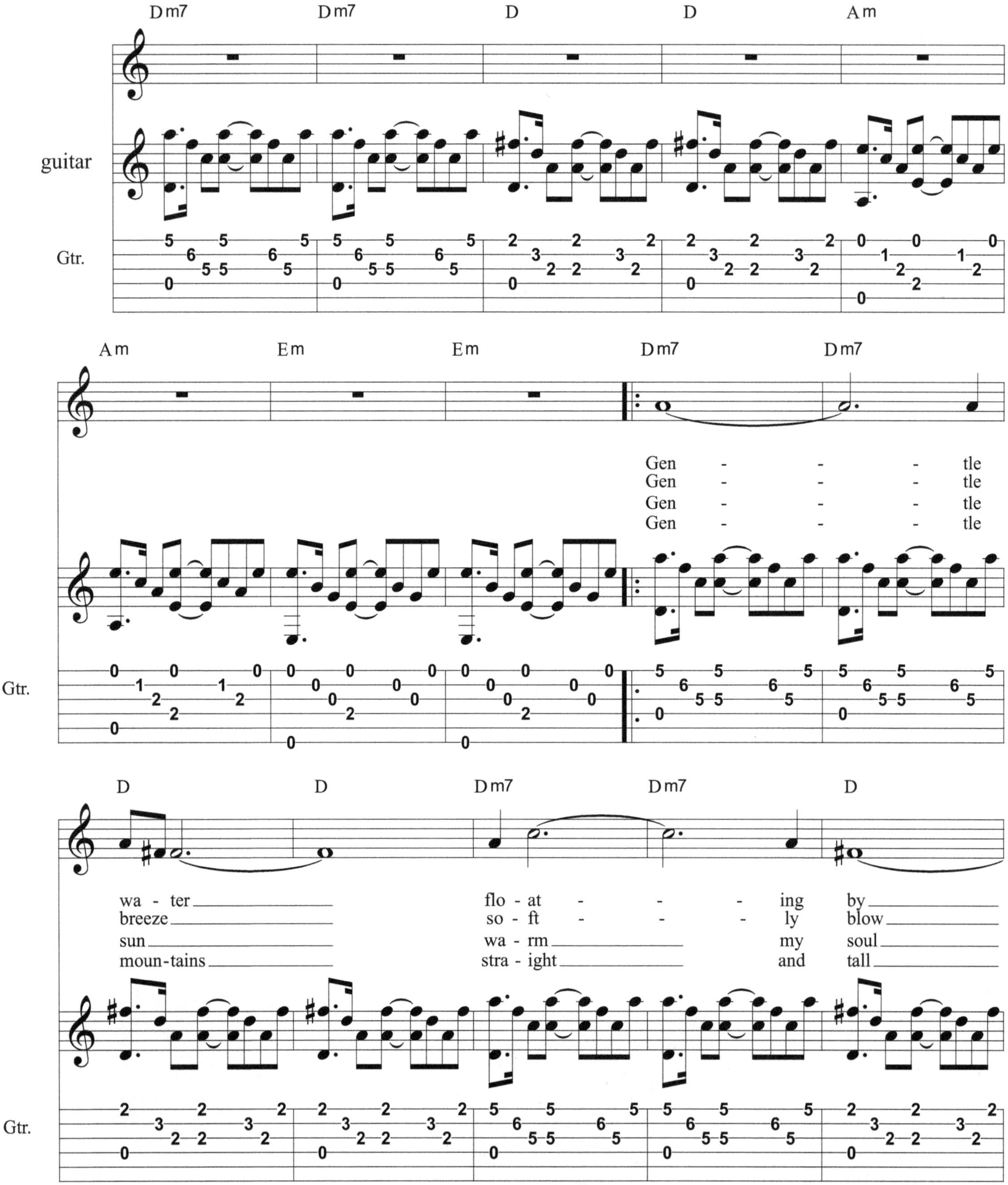
Dm7 Dm7 D D Am
guitar
Gtr.
Am Em Em Dm7 Dm7
Gen - - - tle
Gen - - - tle
Gen - - - tle
Gen - - - tle
Gtr.
D D Dm7 Dm7 D
wa - ter flo - at - - - ing by
breeze so - ft - - - ly blow
sun wa - rm my soul
moun-tains stra - ight and tall
Gtr.

Heal _____ My _____ wounds _____
ca - ress _____ my _____ heart _____
fill me _____ with your light _____
fill me _____ with your strength _____

Teach me _____ to ___ cry _____
help me _____ to ___ grow _____
help make _____ me ___ whole _____
help me _____ face it all _____

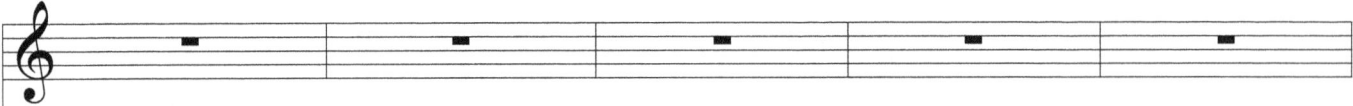

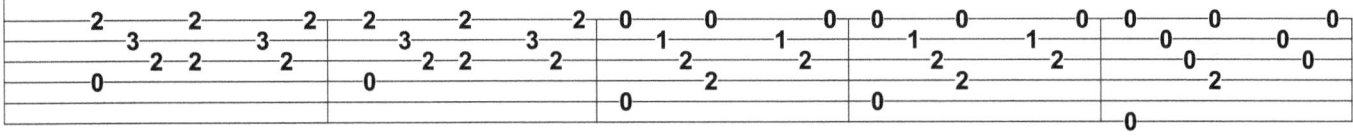
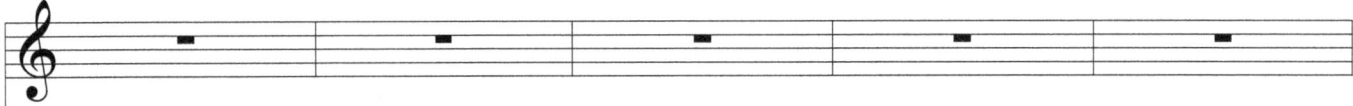

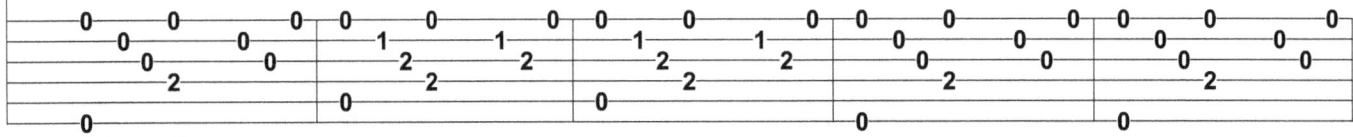
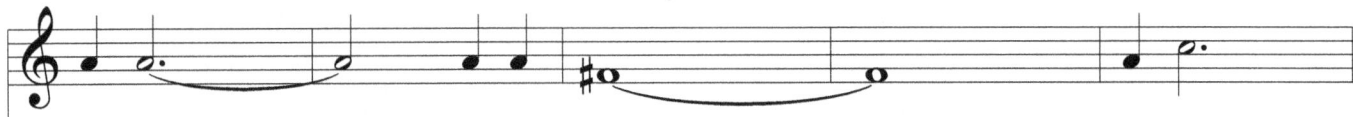

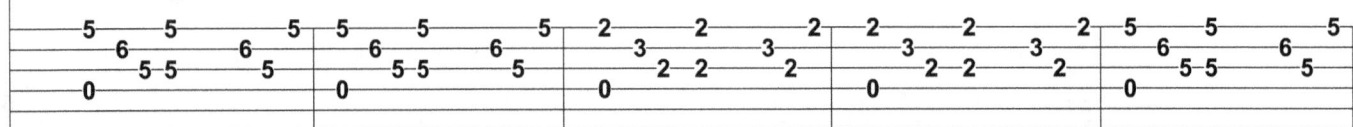

Mo - ther _____ of the earth _____ fa - ther

Dm7 D D Am Am
of the sky love me to -
Gtr.
Em Em Am Am Em
day Al - ways be my guide
Gtr.
Em Dm7 Dm7 D D
mo - ther of the earth
Gtr.

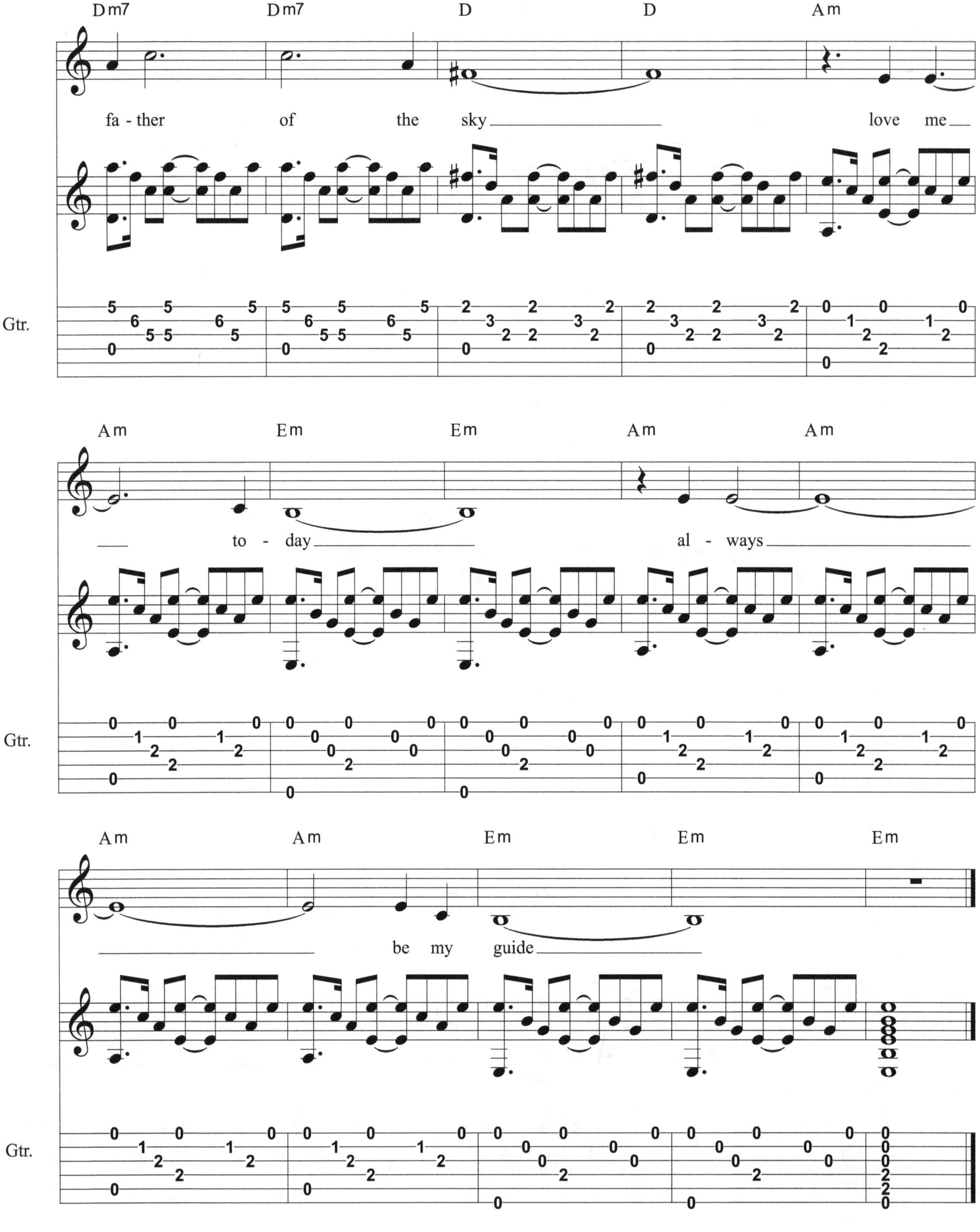
Dm7 Dm7 D D Am
fa - ther of the sky love me
Gtr.
Am Em Em Am Am
to - day al - ways
Gtr.
Am Am Em Em Em
be my guide
Gtr.

# Nobody Knows My Name

Helen Lapakko

I see you

stand-ing there ___ dark-ness is ev-ry-where ___ You turn and look at me ___

Your eyes are an-gry ___ I want to touch you ___ I want to

hold you ___ I want to know you are there

As I grow old - der____ I search for a fa-ther's arms____ Some-one to

ho-ld me____ and keep me safe and warm____ I want him to touch me____

I want him to love me____ I want him to know my___ name

Then the rain be - gins____
Sometimes the sun peeks out____

drip - ping on my skin_____ I want to run and hide_____ to that place I
I want to run and shout_____ twirl around with - out a care_____ arms reach-ing

have in - side_____ Where no one can see me_____ no one can hold me_____
in the air_____ please_ won't you see me_____ please won't you hold me_____

no one can know my_ name_____
please won't you know my_ name_____

Now I stand a - lone____ A child who is full-grown____ Look - ing
I see you stand-ing there____ dark-ness is ev - ry - where____ you turn and

at the world____ no long-er a lit-tle girl____ I want to see me____
look at me____ Your eyes are emp - ty____ you'll nev - er see me____

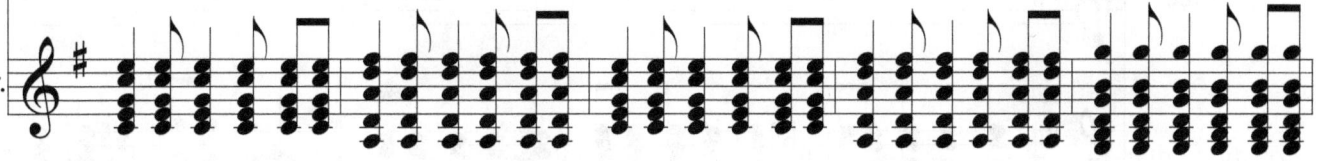

I want to hold me ___ I want to know my ___ name ___
you'll ne-ver hold me ___ you'll ne-ver know my ___ name ___

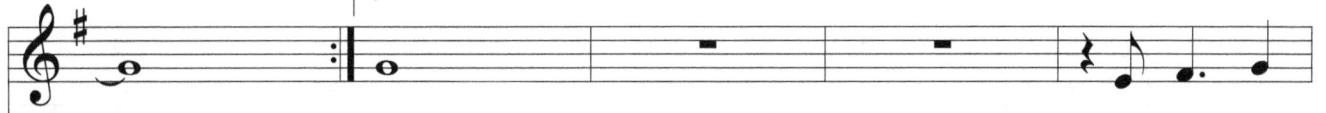
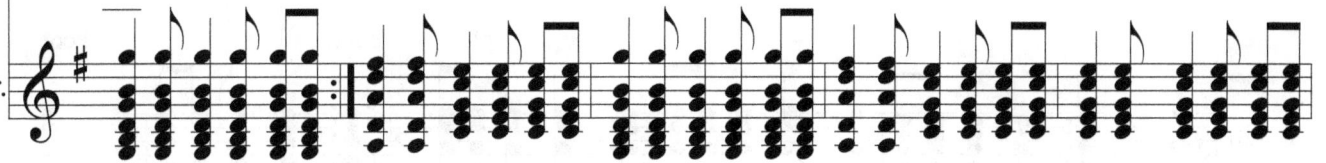

___    you'll nev - er

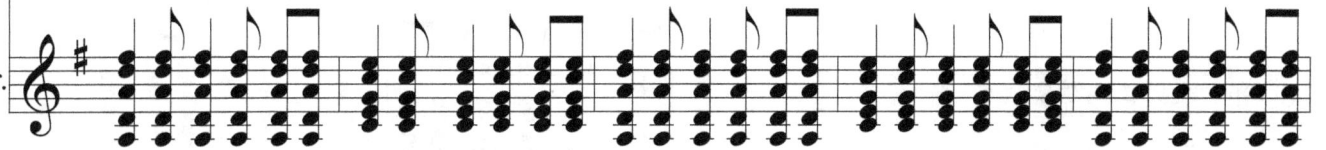

touch me ___ You'll ne - ver love me ___ you'll nev - er know I was

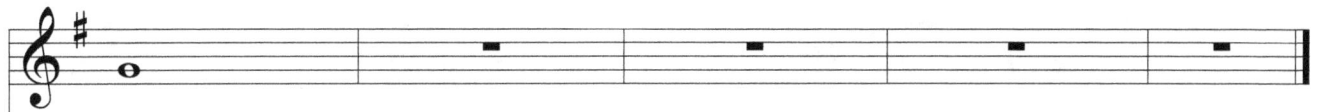
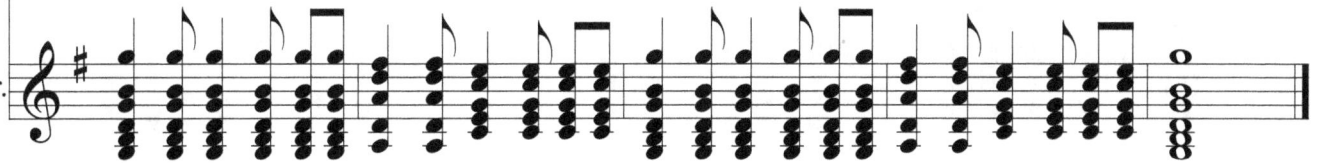

there

# People Come, People Go

Helen Lapakko

Peo ple come Peo - ple

walk-in' on by put-ting on their show

Is that what it means to be to - tal-ly free Well if it

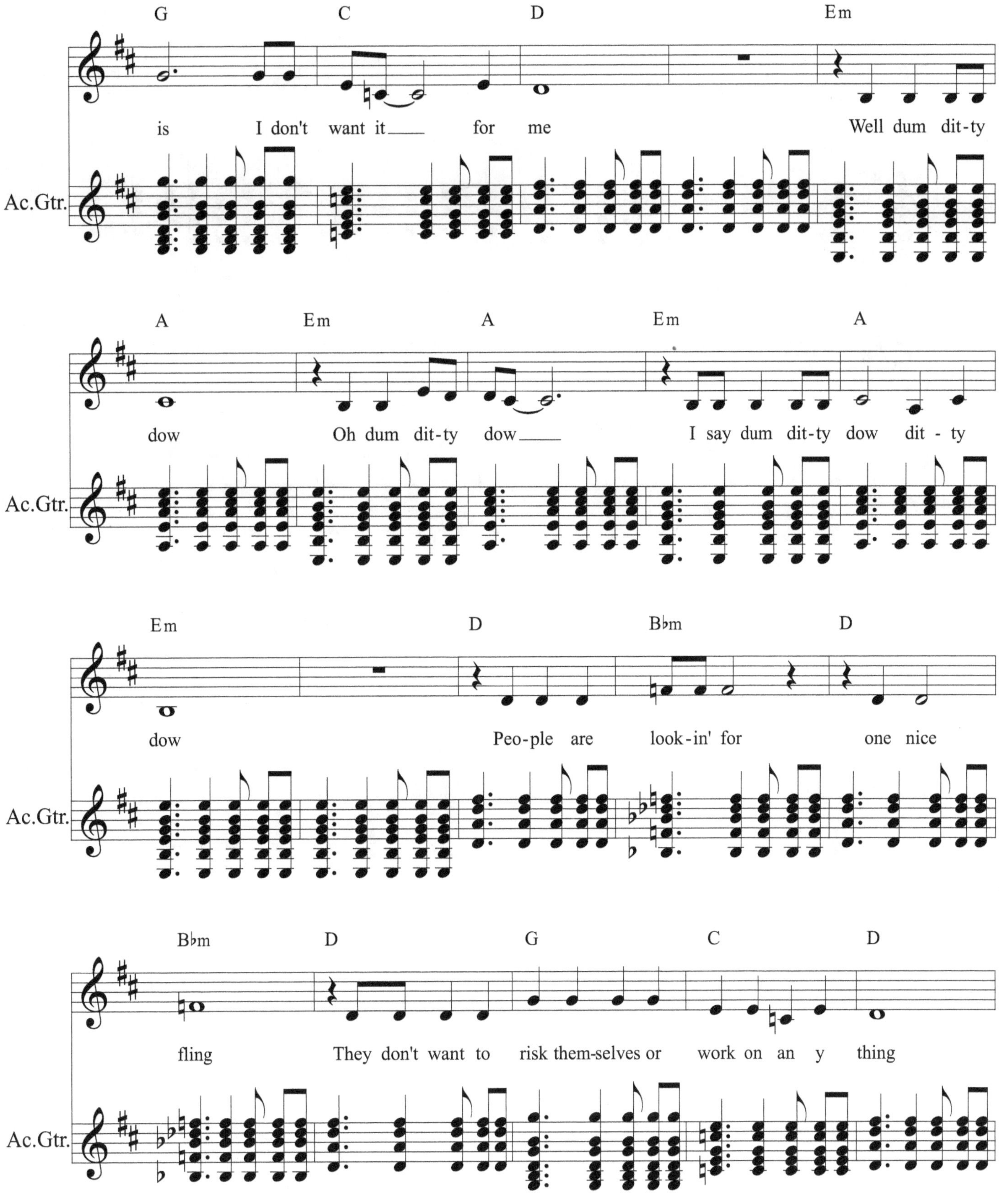
G C D Em
is I don't want it for me Well dum dit-ty
Ac.Gtr.
A Em A Em A
dow Oh dum dit-ty dow I say dum dit-ty dow dit - ty
Ac.Gtr.
Em D B♭m D
dow Peo-ple are look-in' for one nice
Ac.Gtr.
B♭m D G C D
fling They don't want to risk them-selves or work on an y thing
Ac.Gtr.

D Bbm D Bbm D
They go down - town and dance to the band They go down-
Ac.Gtr.
G C D Em
town to find a one night stand Well dum dit-ty
Ac.Gtr.
A Em A Em A
dow Oh dum dit-ty dow I say dum dit-ty dow dit - ty
Ac.Gtr.
Em D Bbm D
dow Where are those people who are like
Ac.Gtr.

me      want-ing      love      and      hap-pi-ness you      see

Where is the      fam-i ly      where has it      gone      what hap-pened to

close-ness  oh      yeah  what's gone      wrong      Well dum  dit-ty

dow      Oh dum dit-ty  dow_____      I say dum dit-ty dow  dit-ty

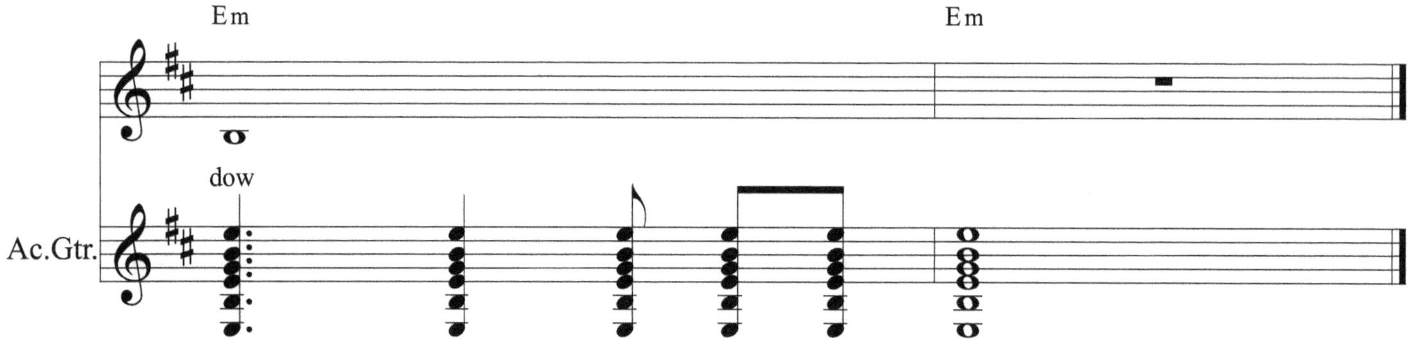
Em
Em
dow
Ac.Gtr.

# Runnin' the Streets

Helen Lapakko

I'm run-nin'_____ the streets run-nin'_____ the streets look - ing for ___ love_____ I'm just

151

look - ing for ___ love

Well ev - ry
The men they

man that ___ I do ___ meet
want me for things that are not right

They think that
They want me

I am so ver - y ver - y sweet
to do dirty deeds of the ___ night

They like my ___
well I'm wary and

eyes so wide and ___ green
scared I stay alone with - in

They are the most
I ___ feel the

152

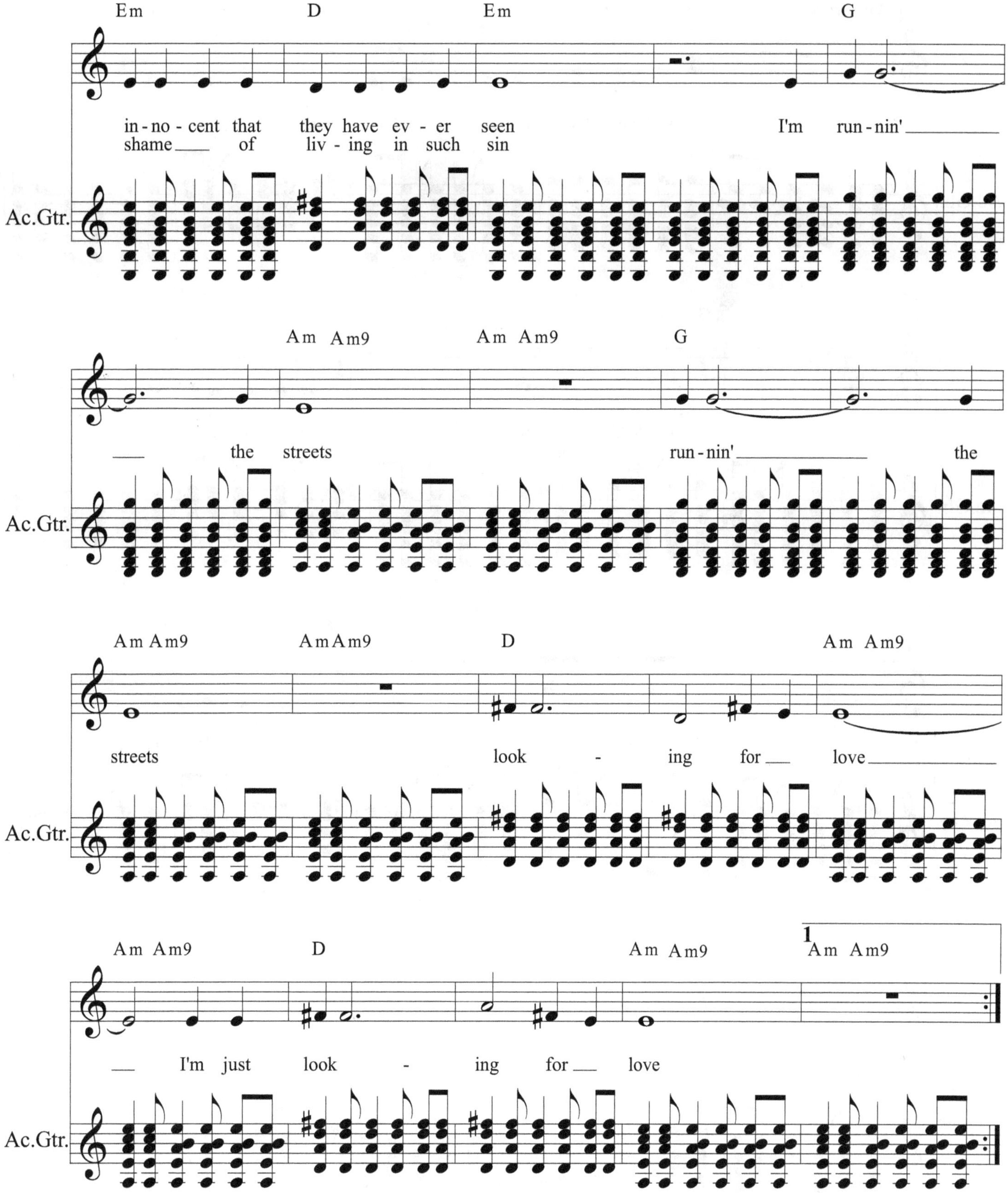
Em D Em G
in - no - cent that they have ev - er seen I'm run - nin'
shame of liv - ing in such sin
Ac.Gtr.
Am Am9 Am Am9 G
the streets run - nin' the
Ac.Gtr.
Am Am9 Am Am9 D Am Am9
streets look - ing for love
Ac.Gtr.
Am Am9 D Am Am9
1
Am Am9
I'm just look - ing for love
Ac.Gtr.

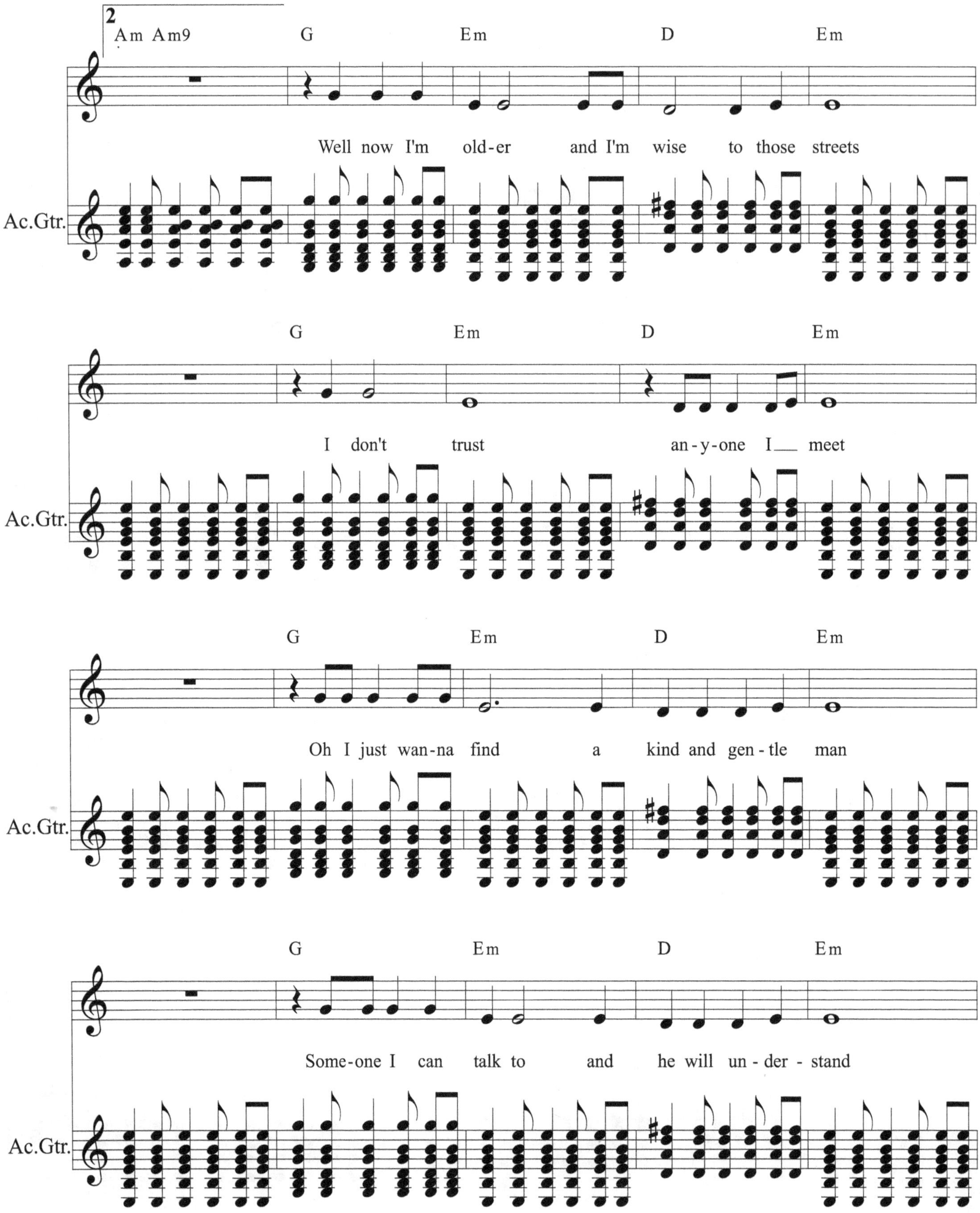
2
Am Am9
G
Em
D
Em
Well now I'm old-er and I'm wise to those streets
Ac.Gtr.
G
Em
D
Em
I don't trust an-y-one I__ meet
Ac.Gtr.
G
Em
D
Em
Oh I just wan-na find a kind and gen-tle man
Ac.Gtr.
G
Em
D
Em
Some-one I can talk to and he will un-der-stand
Ac.Gtr.

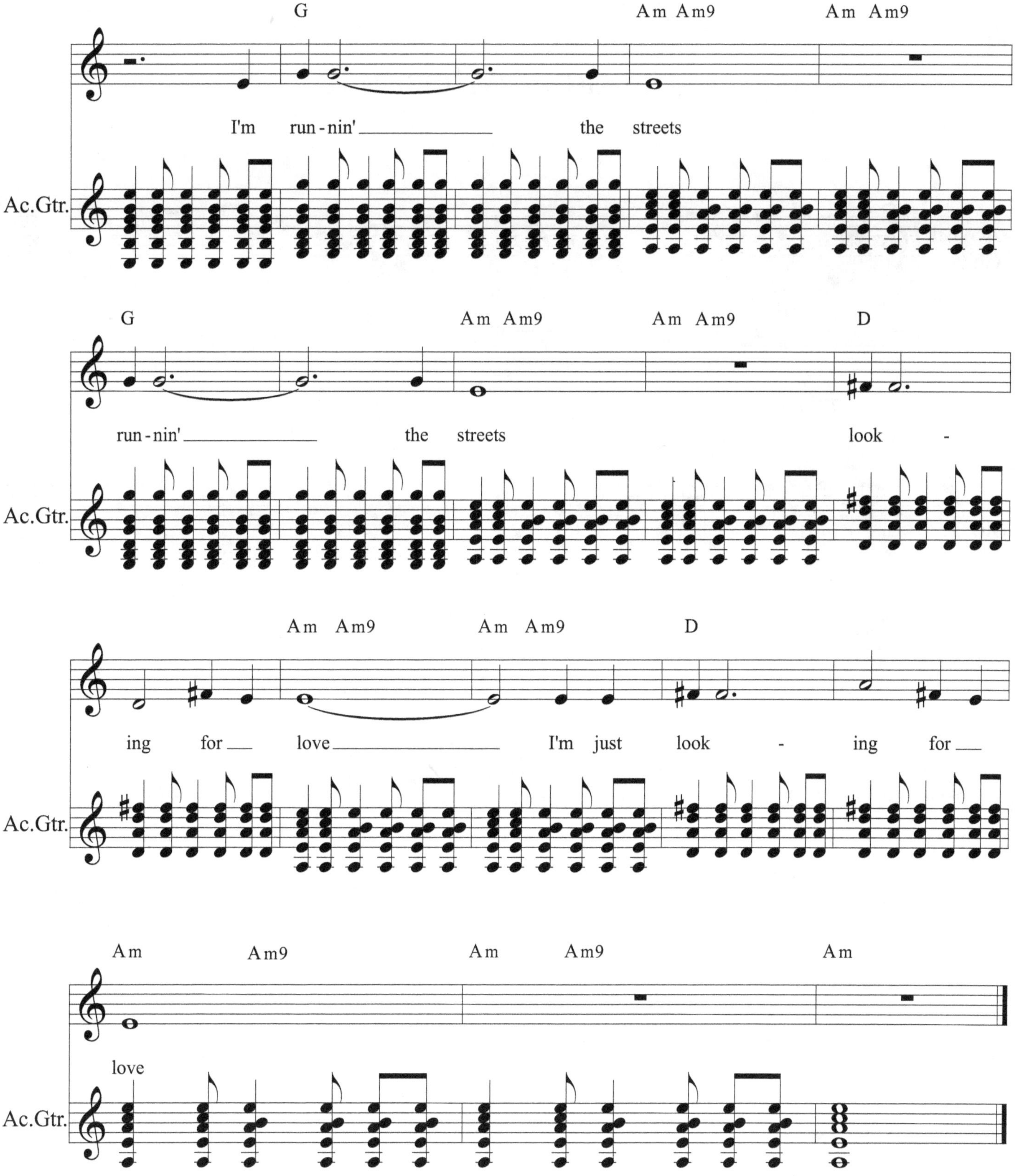
G
Am Am9
Am Am9
I'm run-nin' the streets
Ac.Gtr.
G
Am Am9
Am Am9
D
run-nin' the streets look -
Ac.Gtr.
Am Am9
Am Am9
D
ing for love I'm just look - ing for
Ac.Gtr.
Am
Am9
Am
Am9
Am
love
Ac.Gtr.

# Sunday Afternoon

Helen Lapakko

156

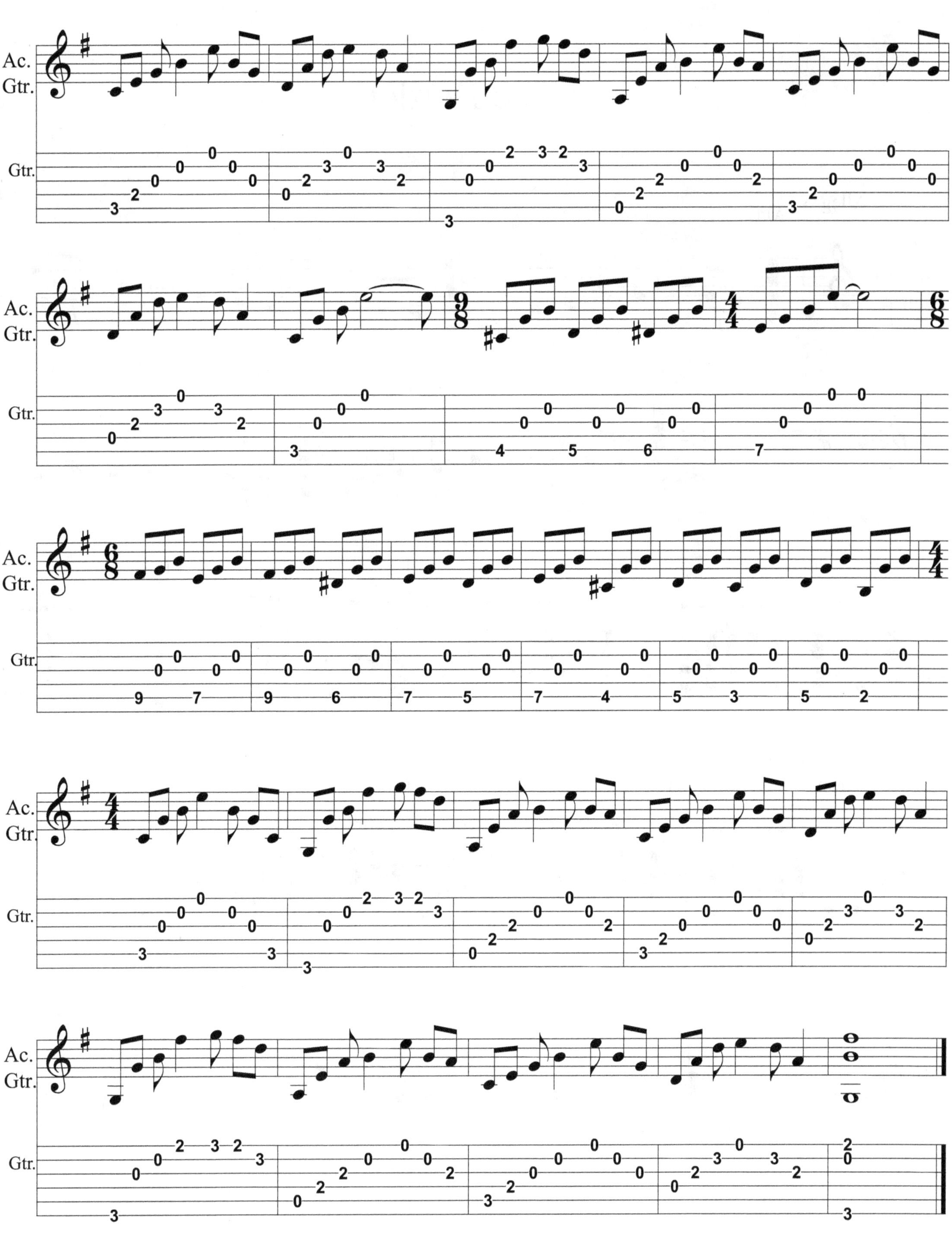
Ac. Gtr.
Gtr.

# The Border

Helen Lapakko

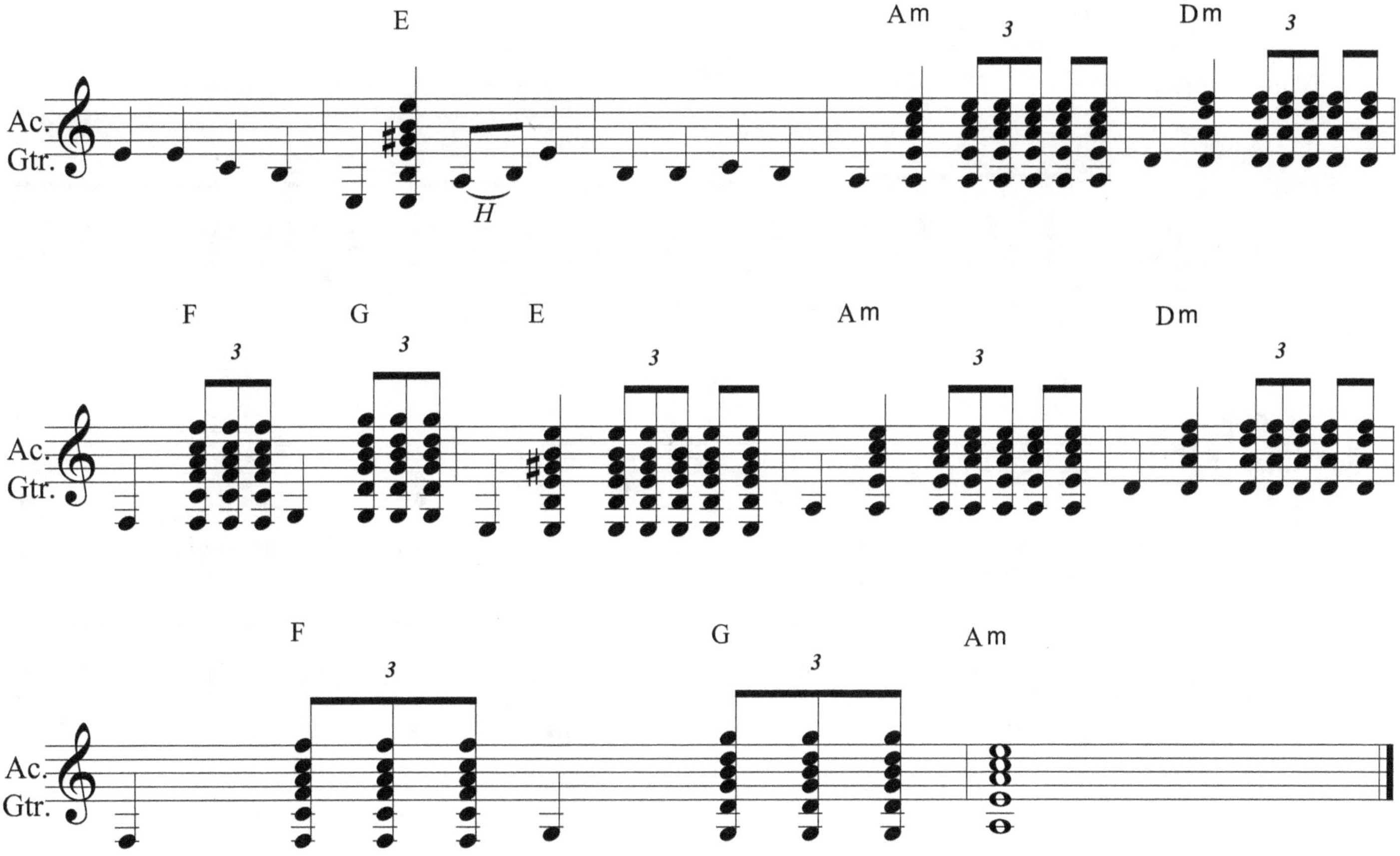
E Am Dm
Ac. Gtr.
H
F G E Am Dm
Ac. Gtr.
F G Am
Ac. Gtr.

# The Old Man

Helen Lapakko

The chords are picked throughout the song.

One day I was walk-ing_____ down the ro-ad_____
We walked to - geth-er_____ along the pa-th_____

I saw an old man car - rying a hea-vy load
He told me sto - ries he made me_____ laugh

He said just fol-low me I know where to go
He said just fol-low me and_____ you will see

I'll bring you___ to that place you need to know
that place where you were meant to___

be
Soon the old man sat down___ by the ro - ad___
Then the old man___ he___ took my ha - nd___

He said I'm___ ti - red of carrying this hea - vy
He said look a - round you at all this___

lo - ad___ He said come sit with me lets rest a
la - nd___ this is___ the___ place where you be -

while · · · · I think it's time for you · · to find your
long · · · · This is the pla - ce where · · you will grow

smile · · · · Now I'm walk-in'_____ down the coun-try
___ · · strong

pa - th_____ · I sing my songs · · some-times I

lau - gh_____ · I laid down my hea-vy load · · I res-ted a

D G D A
while I laid down my hea-vy load and I found my
Ac.Gtr.
D G D A
smile I laid down my hea-vy load and I found my
Ac.Gtr.
D A C A D
smile
Ac.Gtr.

# Thought It Would Last Forever

Helen Lapakko

Why did you go?
It's so___ hard

Why___ did you leave?
when you push me a - way

Now that your gone I must grieve___
Know-ing there's nothing I can say___

I loved you so
I hurt so deep

there's no thin' I would-n't do
I don't wan - na let go

Lyrics below the staves:

I_____ just want ed to be with you_____ I loved your
I thought I did it right I just loved you so_____

smile    your twink-ling eyes    how we would laugh    to -

geth - er _____    We'd sit and talk    the night a -

way    I thought it would last    for - ev-er _____

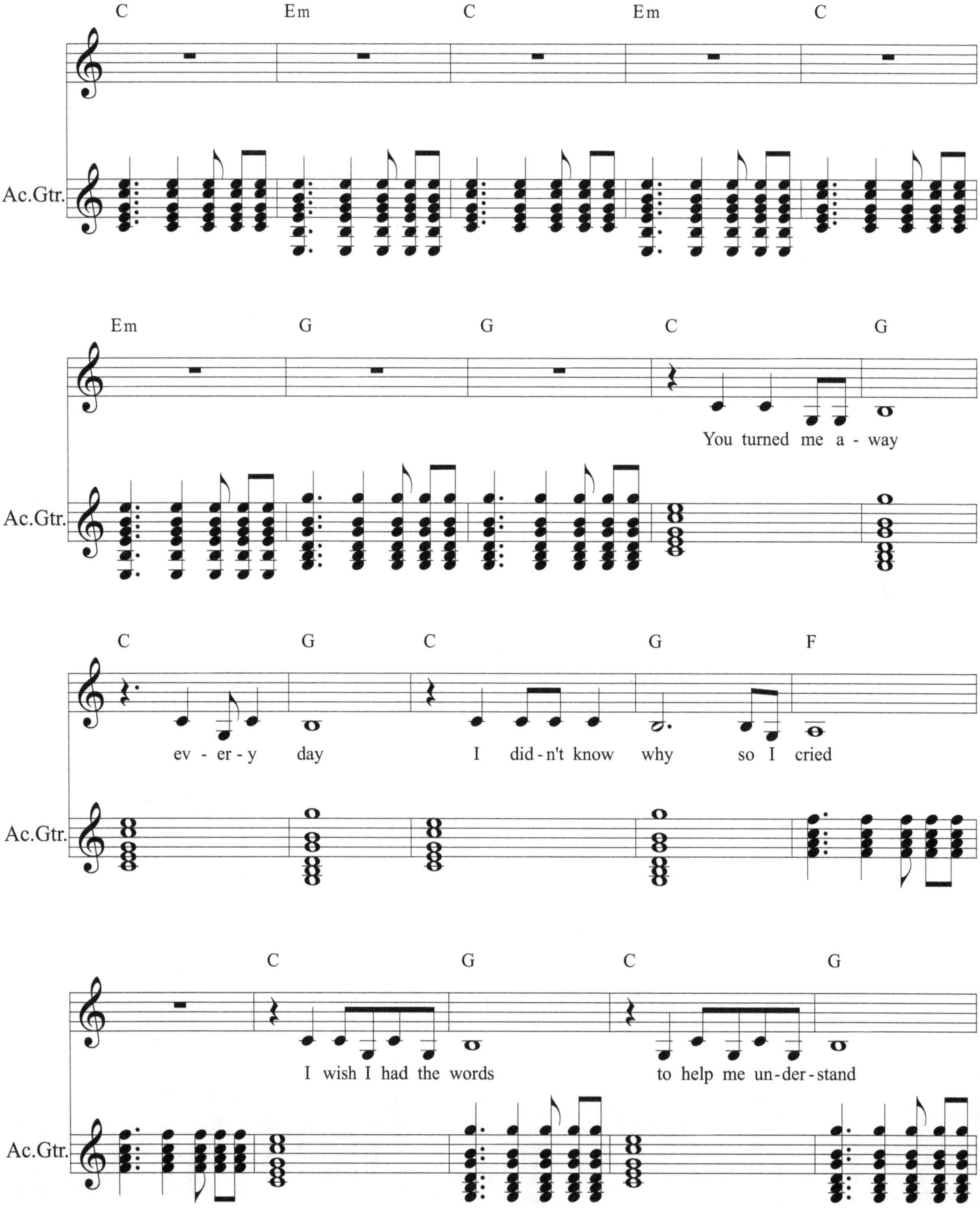
C Em C Em C
Ac.Gtr.
Em G G C G
You turned me a - way
Ac.Gtr.
C G C G F
ev - er - y day I did - n't know why so I cried
Ac.Gtr.
C G C G
I wish I had the words to help me un - der - stand
Ac.Gtr.

Why we can't be to-geth-er a - again _____ I loved your
smile _____ your twink-ling eyes _____ how we would laugh to -
geth - er _____ We'd sit and talk _____ the night a -
way _____ I thought it would last for - ev - er _____

I thought it would last for - ev - er_____ I thought it would

last_____

# Walking Along With a Song

Helen Lapakko

169

# What Rita Coolidge Sang

Helen Lapakko

Lyrics:

Don-ald Byrd sang  street la-dy_____  as if he
Some - times words  build in me_____  a whisper to

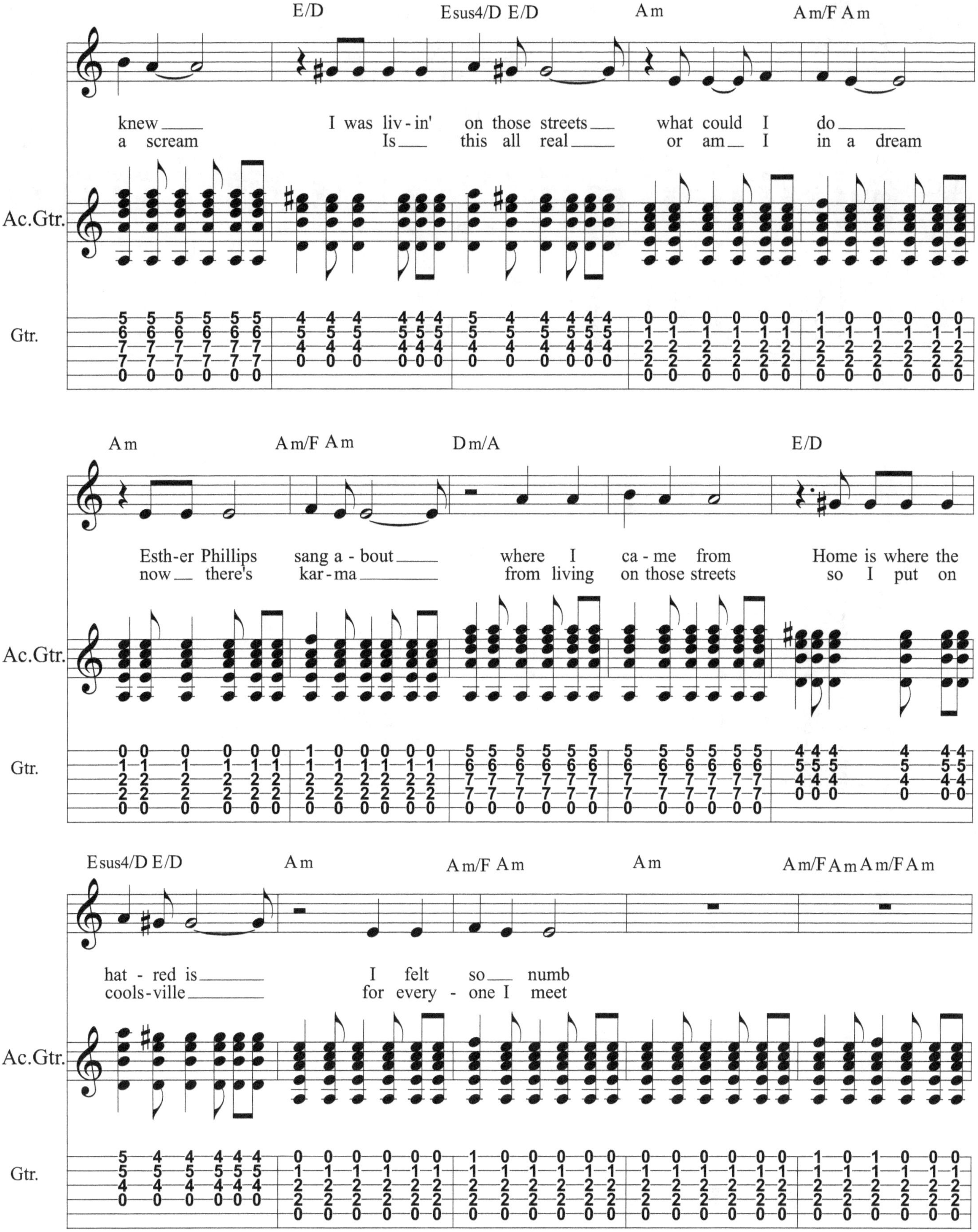
E/D
Esus4/D E/D
Am
Am/F Am
knew I was liv-in' on those streets what could I do
a scream Is this all real or am I in a dream
Ac.Gtr.
Gtr.
Am
Am/F Am
Dm/A
E/D
Esth-er Phillips sang a-bout where I ca-me from Home is where the
now there's kar-ma from living on those streets so I put on
Ac.Gtr.
Gtr.
Esus4/D E/D
Am
Am/F Am
Am
Am/F Am Am/F Am
hat-red is I felt so numb
cools-ville for every-one I meet
Ac.Gtr.
Gtr.

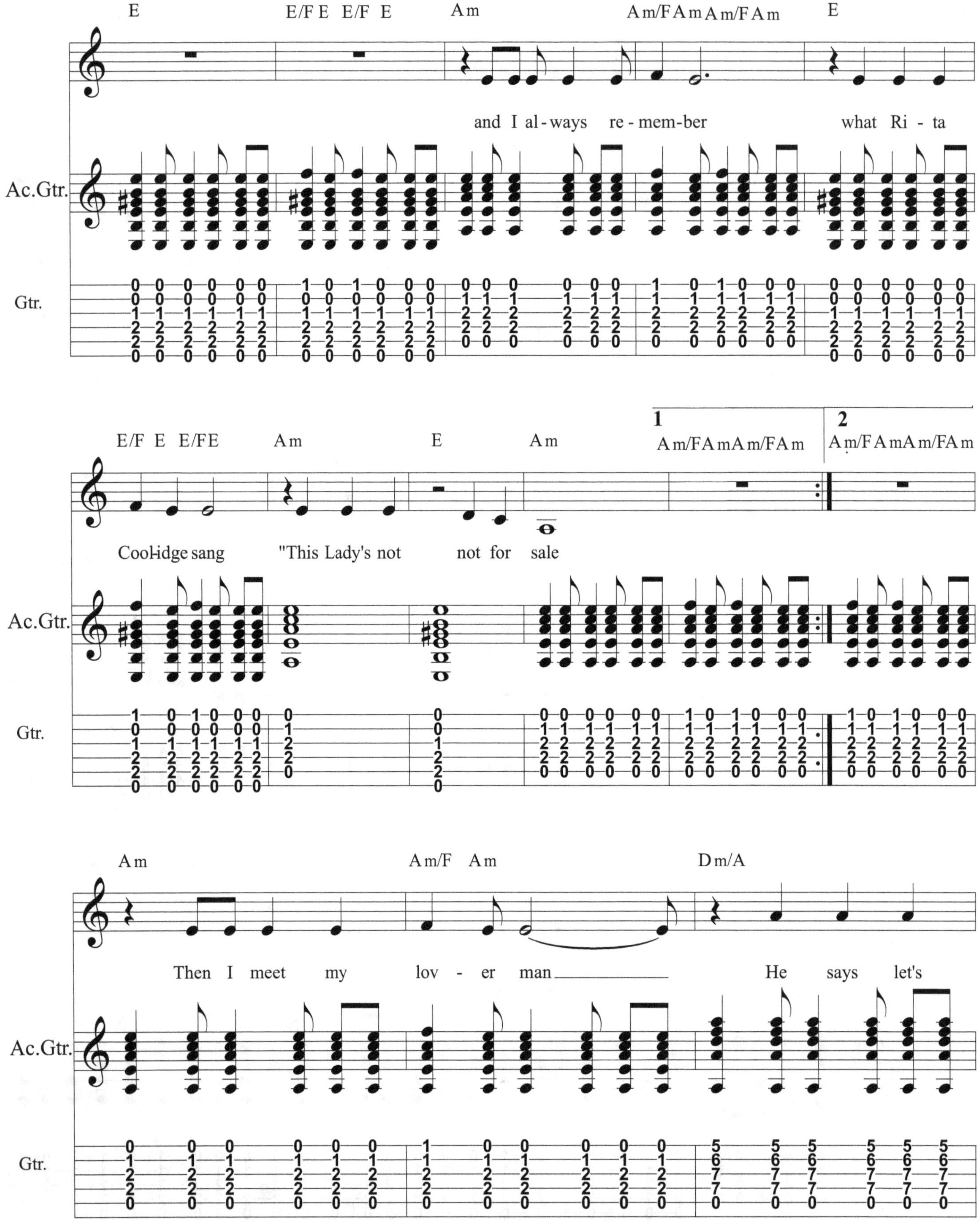
E E/F E E/F E Am Am/F Am Am/F Am E
and I al - ways re - mem - ber what Ri - ta
Ac.Gtr.
Gtr.
E/F E E/F E Am E Am
1 Am/F Am Am/F Am
2 Am/F Am Am/F Am
Cool-idge sang "This Lady's not not for sale
Ac.Gtr.
Gtr.
Am Am/F Am Dm/A
Then I meet my lov - er man He says let's
Ac.Gtr.
Gtr.

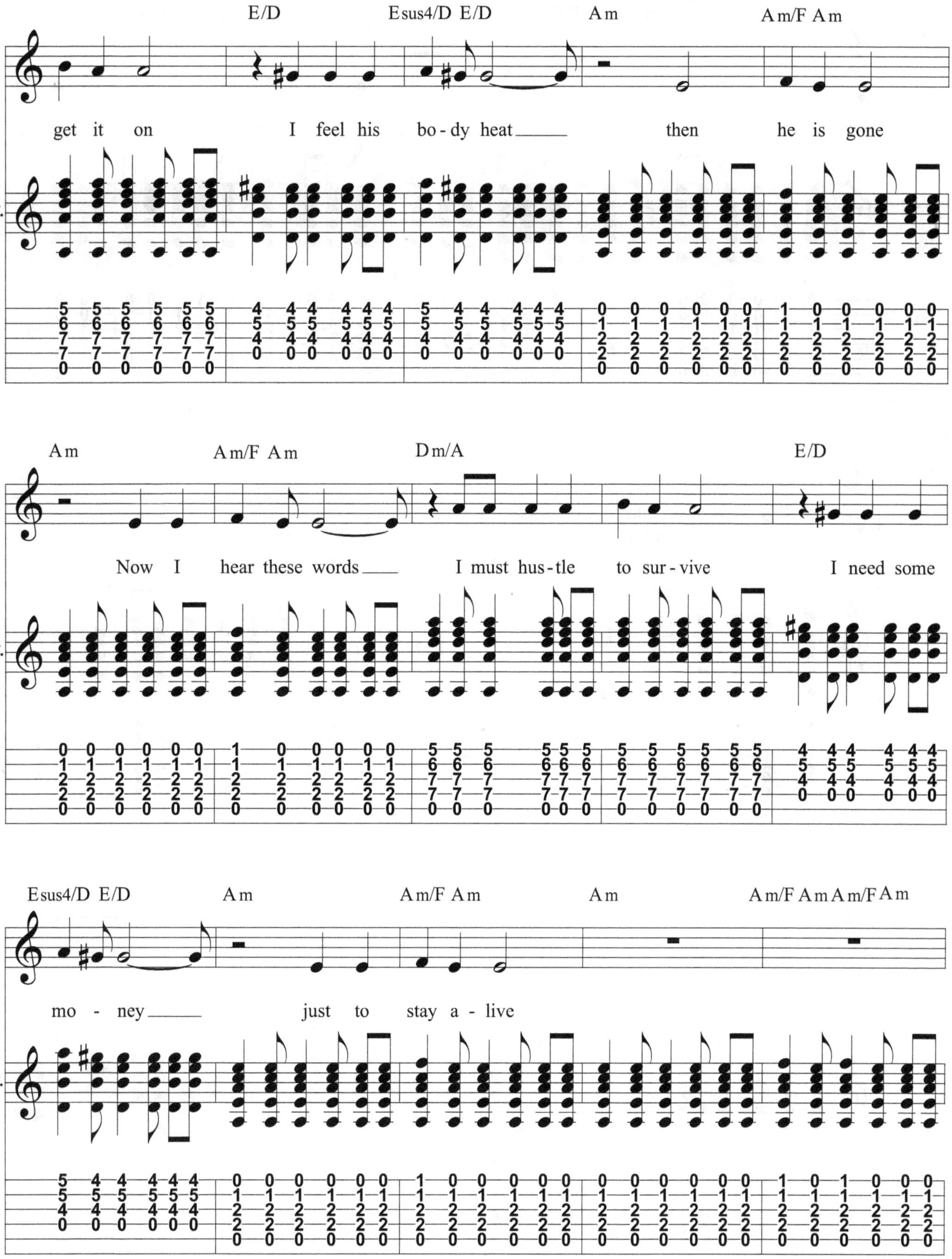
E/D
Esus4/D E/D
Am
Am/F Am
get it on I feel his bo-dy heat then he is gone
Ac.Gtr.
Gtr.
Am
Am/F Am
Dm/A
E/D
Now I hear these words I must hus-tle to sur-vive I need some
Ac.Gtr.
Gtr.
Esus4/D E/D
Am
Am/F Am
Am
Am/F Am Am/F Am
mo - ney just to stay a - live
Ac.Gtr.
Gtr.

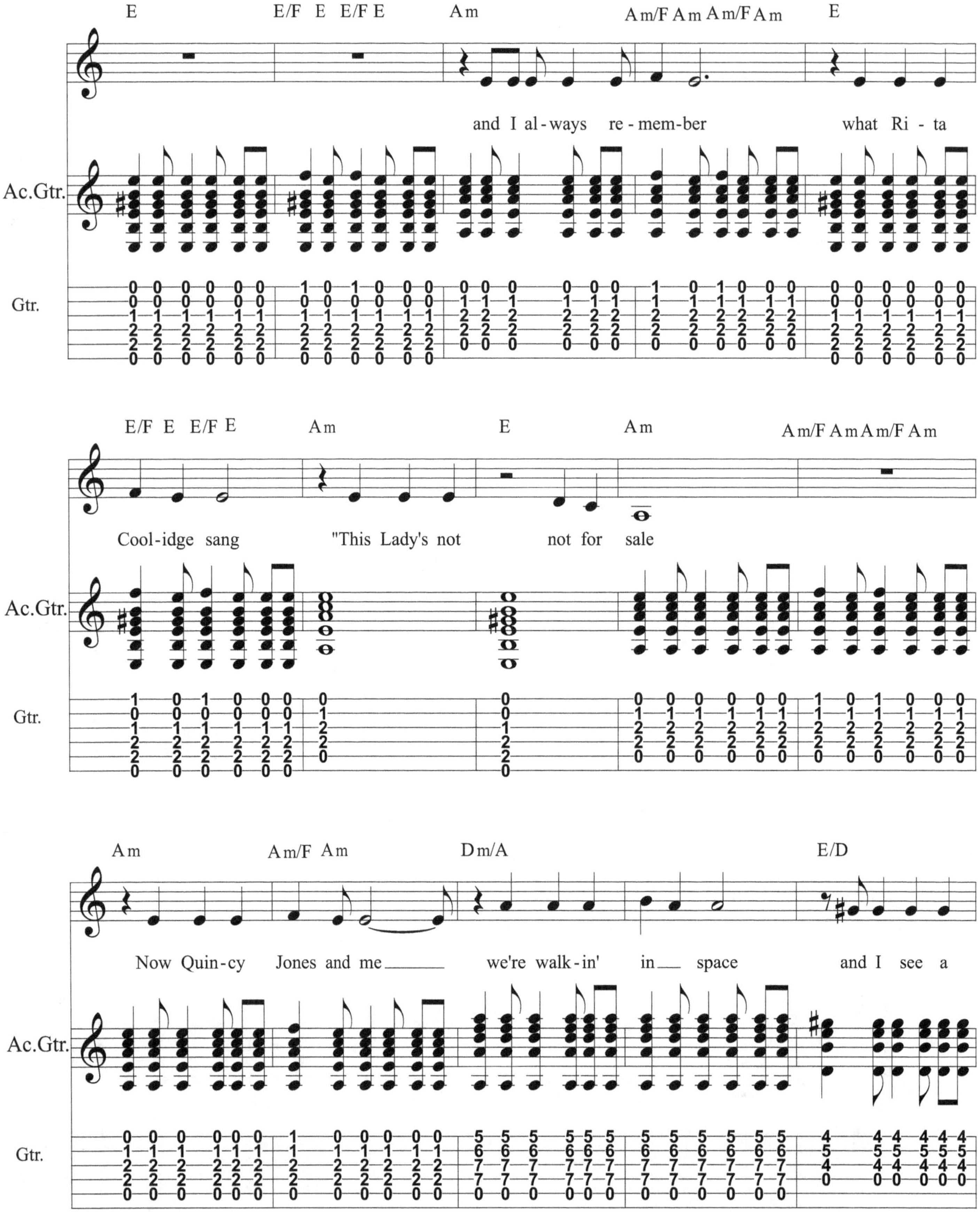
E E/F E E/F E Am Am/F Am Am/F Am E
and I al-ways re-mem-ber what Ri-ta
Ac.Gtr.
Gtr.
E/F E E/F E Am E Am Am/F Am Am/F Am
Cool-idge sang "This Lady's not not for sale
Ac.Gtr.
Gtr.
Am Am/F Am Dm/A E/D
Now Quin-cy Jones and me we're walk-in' in space and I see a
Ac.Gtr.
Gtr.

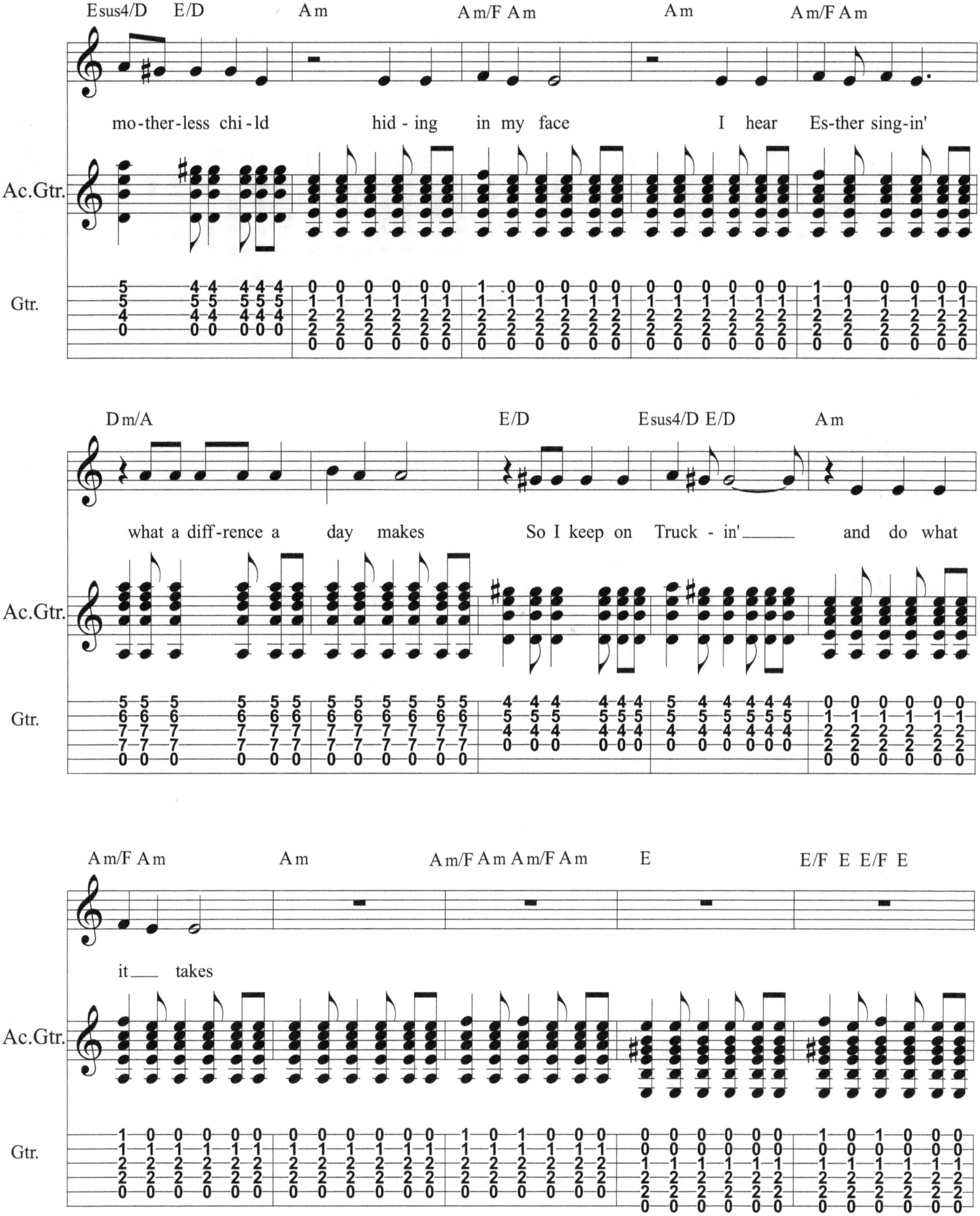
Esus4/D E/D Am Am/F Am Am Am/F Am
mo-ther-less chi-ld hid-ing in my face I hear Es-ther sing-in'
Ac.Gtr.
Gtr.
Dm/A E/D Esus4/D E/D Am
what a diff-rence a day makes So I keep on Truck-in' and do what
Ac.Gtr.
Gtr.
Am/F Am Am Am/F Am Am/F Am E E/F E E/F E
it takes
Ac.Gtr.
Gtr.

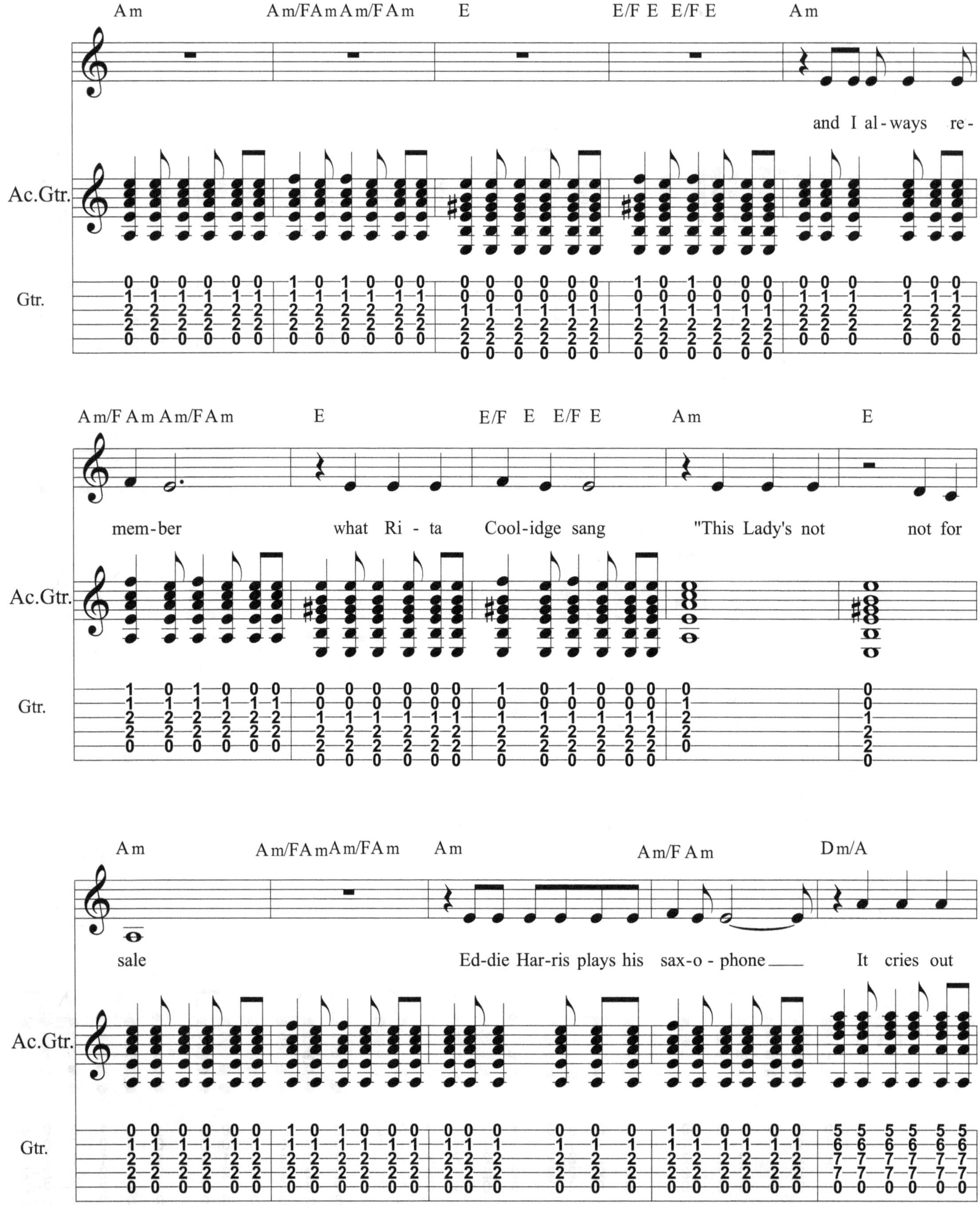
Am Am/F Am Am/F Am E E/F E E/F E Am
and I al-ways re-
Ac.Gtr.
Gtr.
Am/F Am Am/F Am E E/F E E/F E Am E
mem-ber what Ri-ta Cool-idge sang "This Lady's not not for
Ac.Gtr.
Gtr.
Am Am/F Am Am/F Am Am Am/F Am Dm/A
sale Ed-die Har-ris plays his sax-o-phone It cries out
Ac.Gtr.
Gtr.

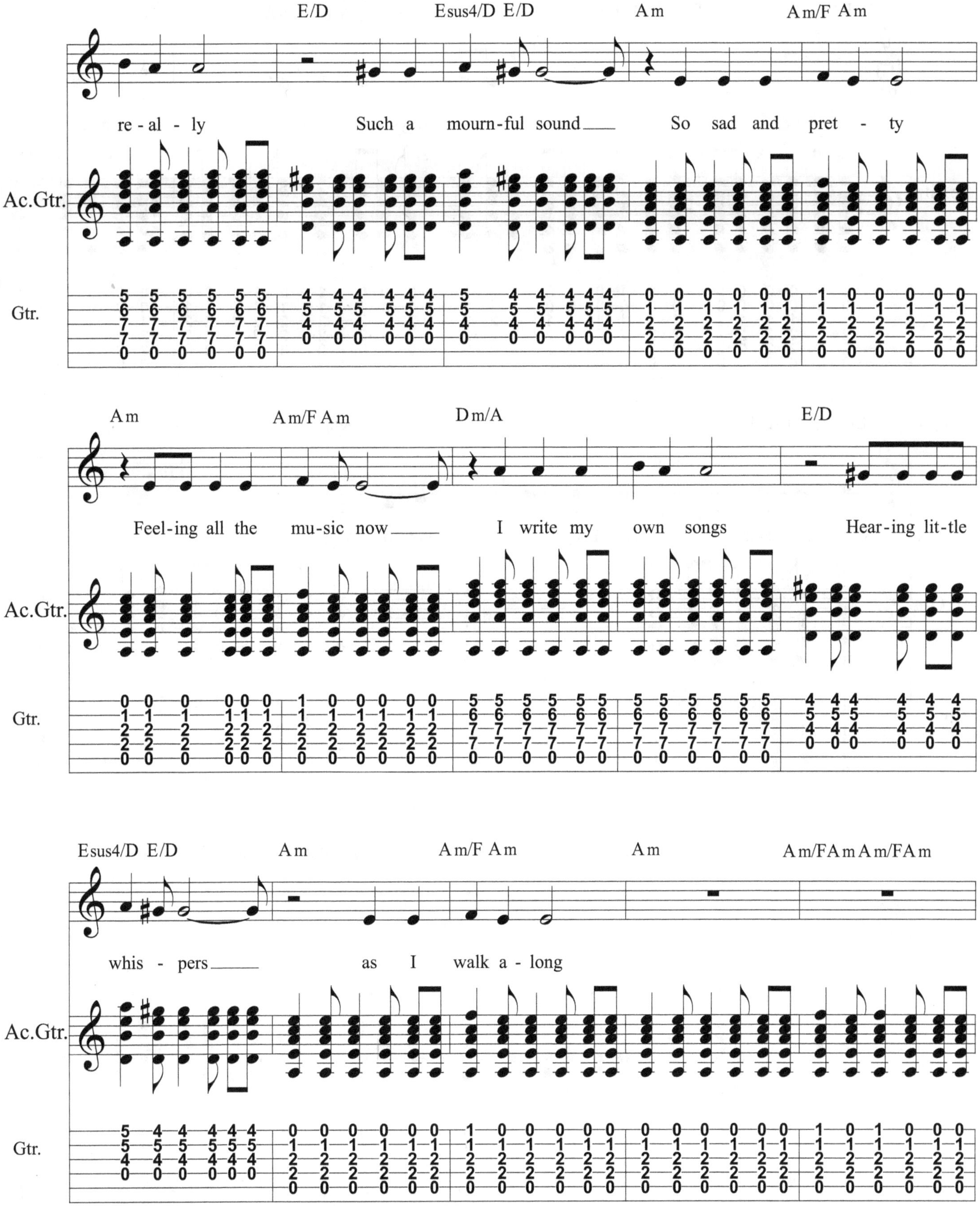
E/D Esus4/D E/D Am Am/F Am
re - al - ly Such a mourn - ful sound So sad and pret - ty
Ac.Gtr.
Gtr.
Am Am/F Am Dm/A E/D
Feel - ing all the mu - sic now I write my own songs Hear - ing lit - tle
Ac.Gtr.
Gtr.
Esus4/D E/D Am Am/F Am Am Am/F Am Am/F Am
whis - pers as I walk a - long
Ac.Gtr.
Gtr.

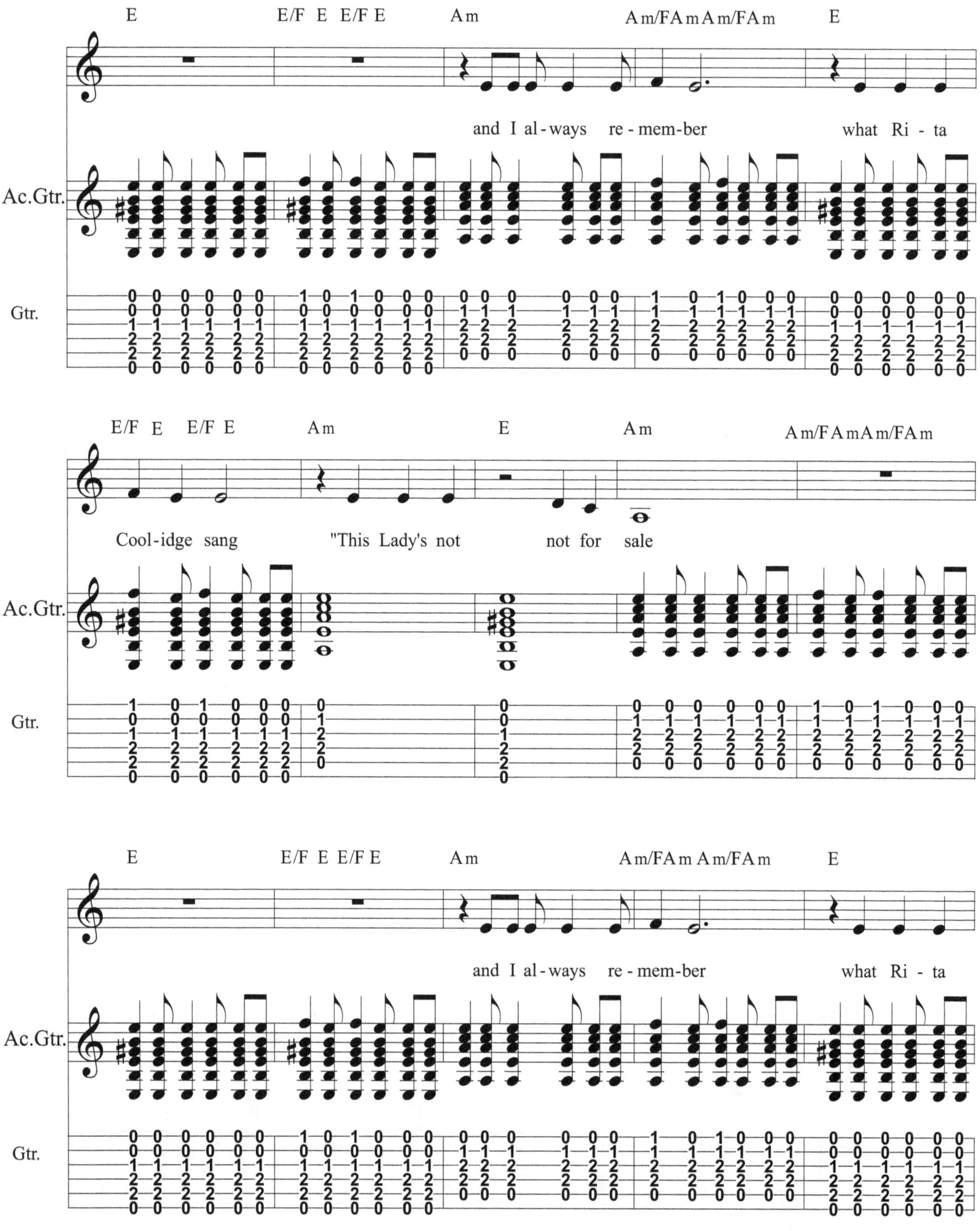
E E/F E E/F E Am Am/FAm Am/FAm E
and I al-ways re-mem-ber what Ri-ta
Ac.Gtr.
Gtr.
E/F E E/F E Am E Am Am/FAm Am/FAm
Cool-idge sang "This Lady's not not for sale
Ac.Gtr.
Gtr.
E E/F E E/F E Am Am/FAm Am/FAm E
and I al-ways re-mem-ber what Ri-ta
Ac.Gtr.
Gtr.

Cool-idge sang        "This Lady's not        not for    sale

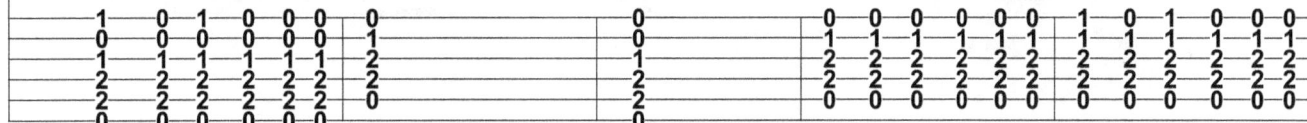

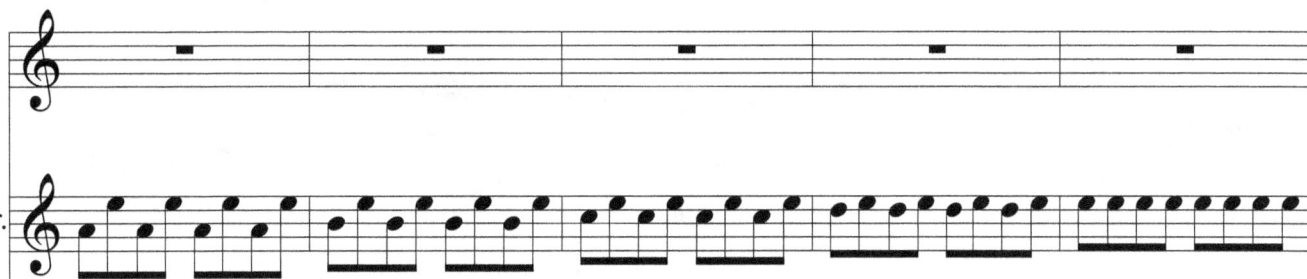

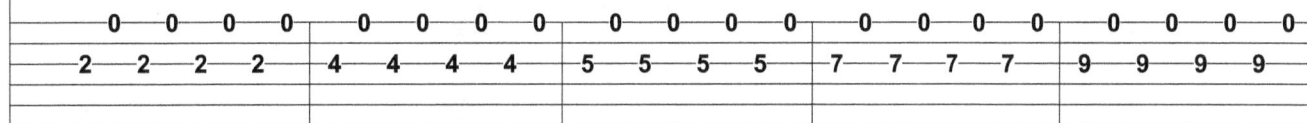

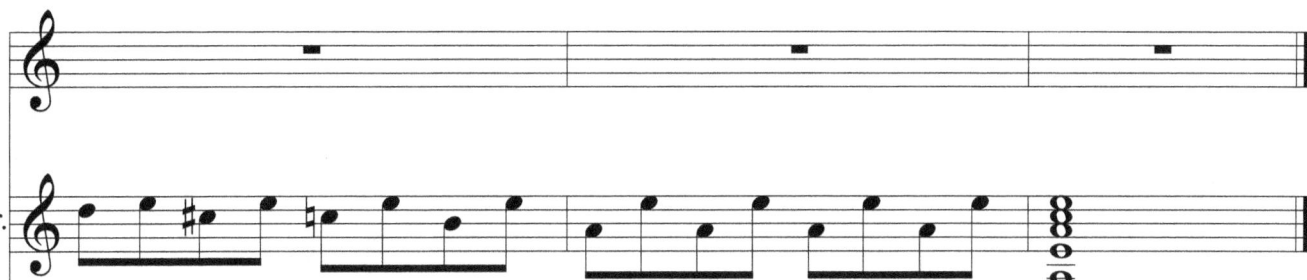

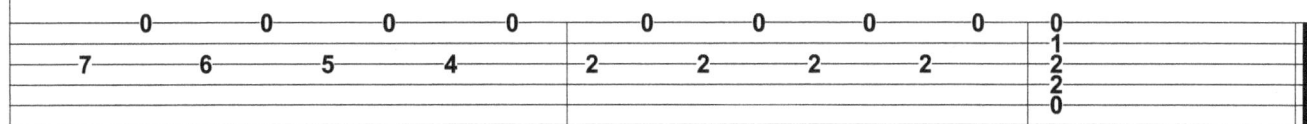

179

# White Note

Helen Lapakko

I see the house with a dark - ened win-dow _____ a white note is stuck to the door

180

I hear____ the laugh-ter_____ and dish - es
I look in the win - dow_____ and see a

clat - ter as din - ner_____ is served
ted - dy bear lying there by the door

I hear the foot-steps_____ run - in' down the stairs on Christ-mas
The rooms are emp-ty_____ with bro-ken pro - mis - es scat-tered____

morn-ing in late Dec - em-ber_____ I hear a lit-tle dog
on_____ the floor_____ Where is the lit-tle girl

barking and chasing a boy and girl around the house
who owns the teddy bear will her dreams still come true

I see the

house with a darkened window _____ a white note is

stuck to the door

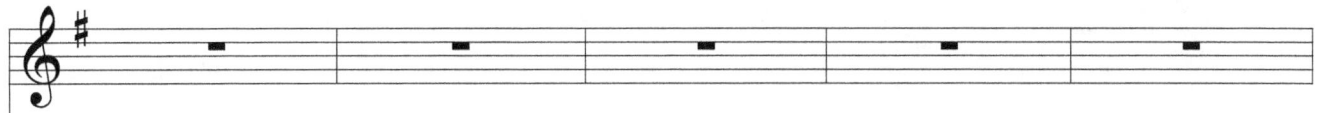

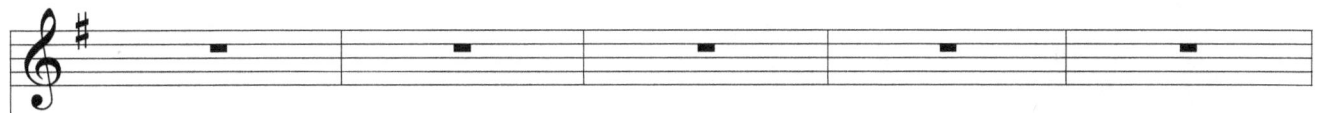

The house it stands    emp-ty    and wait - ing

for the peo-ple to re - turn  I see a

lit-tle boy  tears  on his cheeks  his hand is wav-ing  good-

bye  Now they're gone  are they

hap - py  leav-ing this house that was their home

I see the house with a dark-ened win-dow_____ a white note is stuck to the do-or a white note is stuck to the door

185

# White Powder

Helen Lapakko

You_ came home
I run up the

late_ you seemed so sad_ sud - den - ly you grow
stairs_ to get a - way_ I am so ver - y

ver-y ver - y mad Your eyes are glaz - ed an an - gry
ver - y a - fraid I hear your foot-setps they're com - ing

186

red       I feel that fa - mil - iar       ting - le   of   dread
near       My heart is___ pounding now       so   full   of   fear

White pow - der    white pow - der       on   your

clothes       white pow - der    white pow - der    un - der your   nose

well, soon   you    find me       your fists   are   real
I   grab   the    lamp    -       next   to   the   bed

187

I can - not th - ink___ I can - not feel blow af - ter
I swing with all I have at___ your head now you are

blow I pre - tend I'm not here Your eyes are dark now
da - zed___ I get up and run out___ the front door

the mon-ster is near White pow - der
as fast as I can

white pow - der on your clothes white pow - der white pow - der

188

un - der your nose

Years have pass - ed you're fin - ally

gone___ Now I___ know I did no - thing wrong

now I'm at peace    I'm fin - ally safe ___    no lon-ger do I

see ___    mon-sters in that face    White pow - der

white pow - der    on your clothes    white pow - der    white pow - der

un - der your nose    white pow - der    white pow - der    un - der your nose           white pow - der      white pow - der      un - der your nose

# Will You Ever Return

Helen Lapakko

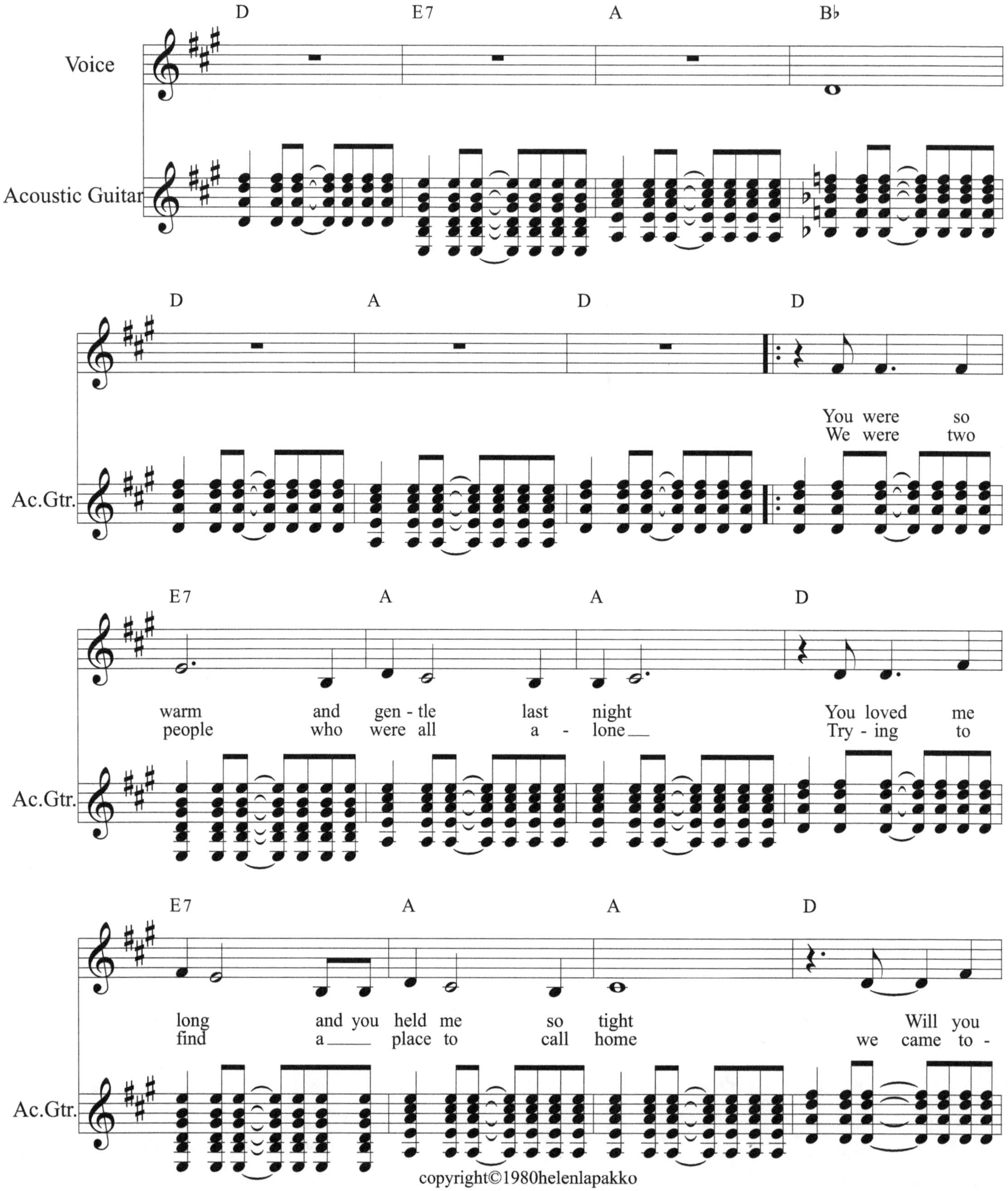
Voice
Acoustic Guitar
Ac.Gtr.
D E7 A B♭
D A D D
E7 A A D
E7 A A D
You were so
We were two
warm and gen - tle last night
people who were all a - lone
You loved me
Try - ing to
long and you held me so tight
find a place to call home
Will you
we came to -

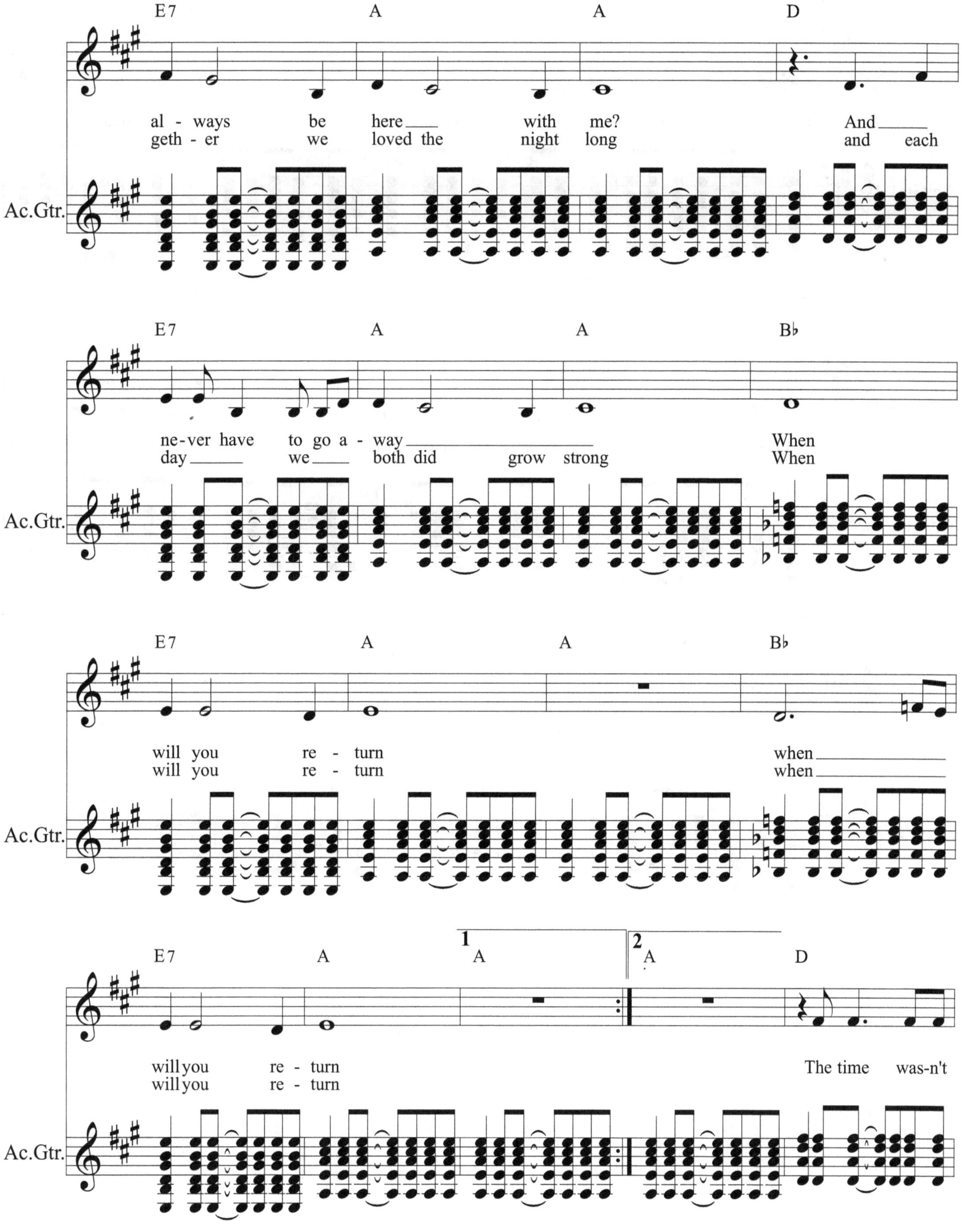
E7 A A D
al - ways be here with me? And
geth - er we loved the night long and each
Ac.Gtr.
E7 A A B♭
ne-ver have to go a - way When
day we both did grow strong When
Ac.Gtr.
E7 A A B♭
will you re - turn when
will you re - turn when
Ac.Gtr.
1 2
E7 A A A D
will you re - turn The time was-n't
will you re - turn
Ac.Gtr.

Line 1 lyrics: right for me ___ and you We tried hard to

Line 2 lyrics: make it Oh, you know that it's true But some-thin' kept

Line 3 lyrics: say-in' that it was just wrong That's why I'm

Line 4 lyrics: sing-in' to you this sad song When

Chords line 1: E7 A A D
Chords line 2: E7 A A D
Chords line 3: E7 A A D
Chords line 4: E7 A A B♭

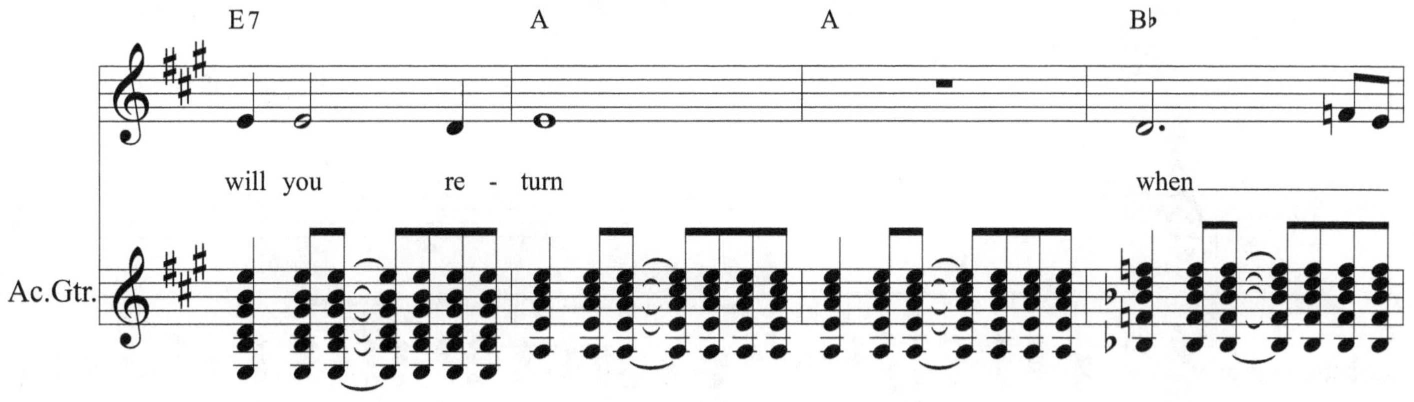
E7
A
A
B♭
will you re - turn when
Ac.Gtr.

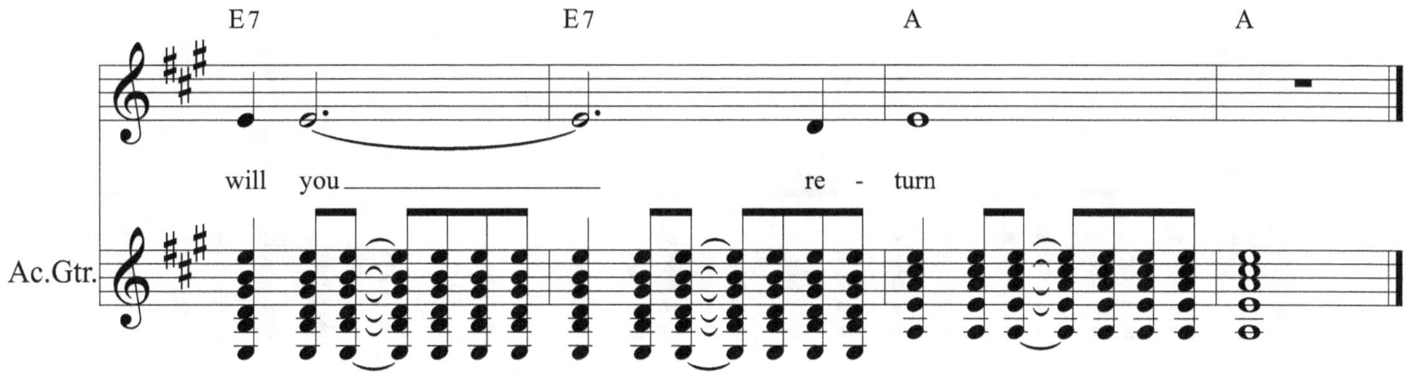
E7
E7
A
A
will you re - turn
Ac.Gtr.

# Young Boy

Helen Lapakko

Well, how ___ ya do - in' young boy ___ how ___ are
you to-day ___ Yes, how ya do - in' young boy ___ can ___ I
have my way ___ ev-ry ___ one Watched as you ___
you looked so good to me ___

walked and strolled a - round          Ev-ry la - dy    in   the place_____
so_____ late last night          walk - in'____ down the street_____

they could - n't make a    sound          You held your head so
with____ your pants so    tight          oh, we____ had____

per - fect - ly_____ your hair___ was just right          Your clothes were a
so  much fun_____ you brought me such joy          they____ say it's

per - fect fit_____ You were real-ly out of sight
always bet - ter_____ with____ a____ young boy

Well how ya do-in' young boy how are you to-day

yes, how ya do-in' young boy Can I have my way

Oh you sweet young thing come play with

me I know that you can go long-er than

Lyrics:

three

I like your lov - in' when

the sun goes down cause your the ver - y best

there is in town Well, how ya

do - in' young boy how are you to - day Yes, how ya

do - in' young boy    can___ I    have my way___

Well, how___    ya    do - in' young boy    how___ are    you to-day___

Yes, how    ya    do - in' young boy    can___ I    have my wa    -

y

9781946195456